# Incomes Policy

*Barbara Wootton*

# Incomes Policy

*AN INQUEST AND A PROPOSAL*

DAVIS-POYNTER
LONDON

First published in 1974 by Davis-Poynter Ltd
20 Garrick Street London WC2E 9BJ

ISBN 0 7067 0166 6

Printed by
Cambridge University Press
Cambridge

# Contents

|  |  | Page |
|---|---|---|
| PREFACE | | 9 |
| I | The background story | 11 |
| II | The trend towards compulsion and the Labour Government's experiment, 1966-1970 | 32 |
| III | Compulsion under the Conservatives: The Counter-Inflation Acts, 1972 and 1973 | 61 |
| IV | Outline proposal for an Incomes Gains Tax | 84 |
| V | Incomes Gains Tax: Treatment of special cases | 99 |
| VI | Incomes Gains Tax: Some loose ends | 135 |
| VII | The case for an Incomes Gains Tax | 152 |
| SUMMARY OF PROPOSALS | | 169 |
| INDEX | | 173 |

# Acknowledgements

I am glad to express my thanks for permission to use quotations as follows:

To the *Sunday Times* for extracts from an article by Robert Lacey in the *Sunday Times Magazine* (for 1 October 1972).
To *The Times* for passages from articles by Dr. Jeffrey Gray (8 September 1972), Mr. Reginald Maudling (12 September 1972), Mr. Richard Crossman (13 September 1972), and Mr. Bernard Levin (1 November 1973).
To the Working Together Campaign for extracts from their study of *Some Aspects of National Job Evaluation* (January 1973).

I also wish to record with gratitude my indebtedness to the Joseph Rowntree Social Service Trust for research and clerical assistance, which is the more appreciated in that it was unsolicited; and to Vera Seal, who has typed and re-typed successive versions of this book, and has read and re-read them with a watchful eye for errors and omissions. For those mistakes that have escaped detection I alone, of course, must take responsibility.

I have used a number of abbreviations in this book, which are given below:

CBI  Confederation of British Industry
IGT  Incomes Gains Tax
PIB  National Board for Prices and Incomes
SEB  Special Exemptions Board (in connection with Incomes Gains Tax)
TUC  Trades Union Congress

# Preface

Since I published *The Social Foundations of Wage Policy,* almost 20 years ago, it has often been suggested to me that a revised edition of this book would be opportune. Circumstances, however, have changed so much during the intervening years that it no longer seems practicable to put new wine into this old bottle. In the pages that follow I have therefore attempted to begin all over again.

This is not a book for professional economists, nor is its author entitled to be so described. Over the years, the focus of my interest has shifted from the economic to the social, and it is only because incomes policy, besides being of personal concern to everybody, straddles the frontier between these two areas, that I have, perhaps rashly, ventured to trespass into economic territory. But the result must be read as a non-specialist essay for non-specialists.

It is also a book about half a problem. The other half relates to price control. Apart from a few observations in the closing pages, I have not dared to tackle this much more difficult problem, but have simply assumed throughout that others would be struggling with it, if and when my policy should be adopted. But I do claim that my proposed Incomes Gains Tax would exercise a powerful restraint upon prices by eliminating the ill-gotten gains of those who make money out of inflation and so have a vested interest in its continuance.

Early sketches of the ideas developed in the pages that follow first appeared in articles published as long as three years ago (the fullest in the *Listener* for 1

April 1971). That it has taken so long to develop my proposals even as far as this has been due, not only to the author's heavy commitments elsewhere, but even more to the need to keep pace with the dizzy succession of changes in public policy. Even as this book goes to press, a Labour government is proposing to combine a statutory control of prices with a voluntary incomes policy. If, contrary to my expectation, that policy is still working successfully when these pages appear in print, that will be more than sufficient compensation for the fact that this book will once more have been overtaken by events. Even so, no one knows what the future may hold, and the day may yet come when it will be handy to have a long-term non-inflationary plan for regulating the distribution of income tucked away somewhere in the files.

B.W.

May 1974

# I

## The Background Story

DURING the past half-century in this country we have lived through a series of astonishing economic revolutions — revolutions in public attitudes and expectations, in economic theories and in economic policy. All are mutually connected, but not in any clear logical sequence.

Perhaps the most radical and remarkable of these innovations has been the almost universal conviction that, come what come may in the economic situation, it is a law of nature that everybody's (or almost everybody's) income ought to be increased regularly every year. Pensioners and others not enjoying the benefit of collective bargaining, who were at first ignored by this principle, may have to be content with increases designed only to keep pace with the cost of living at yearly or six-monthly intervals. But right down to the critical winter of 1973-4 it had become an accepted axiom that, at least for everyone in active employment, not only money incomes, but also actual standards of living, should improve annually. In February 1972, when the ink was barely dry on Lord Wilberforce's settlement of that year's coal dispute, it was announced that the next round of wage negotiations in the mining industry would begin in the following July; and, as everybody knows, it was the failure of those negotiations which resulted in the miners' overtime ban and strike less than two years later.

Throughout the whole post-war period wage claims have succeeded one another in a regular series of 'rounds', and their success is demonstrated by the

Department of Employment's figures. From mid-1956 to mid-1972 the official index of weekly wage rates for adult male manual workers (31 January 1956 = 100) rose from 105.5 to 244.1,[1] that is by over 130%, while manual workers' annual earnings showed a similarly unbroken rise. In September 1968 the Department of Employment's new survey of earnings, giving wider coverage of both manual and non-manual workers, showed the median weekly earnings of all full-time adult males to have risen from £23.6 in September 1968 to £38.4 in April 1973.[2] Indeed so firmly established was the doctrine of higher still and higher, that when Mr. Anthony Barber introduced his emergency 'mini-budget' in the supposedly desperate circumstances of December 1973, the most ominous prospect that he foresaw was that 'while the [oil] shortage lasts we might have to accept the living standards of, say, a year ago rather than the improvement which we could have expected in the year ahead'.[3] A temporary standstill due only to the single factor of oil shortage was, it seems, the worst that could be contemplated.

Hardly anyone who has not reached the late fifties can have a clear personal memory of the novelty of this assumption that every year, as it passes, should automatically put more money into almost every pocket. Yet it is a fact that things were once very different. In the nineteen-twenties, when I worked in what was then the Joint Research Department of the Trades Union Congress and the Labour Party, our slogan was 'Not a penny off the pay, not a minute on the day'. Nor were we even very successful in this defensive struggle merely to maintain the *status quo*. In 1921 over 7,244,000 wage-earners lost £6,074,600 a week in wage reductions, while in the following

1. HMSO Annual Abstract of Statistics, 1965, and 1973.
2. Department of Employment Gazette, May 1969, and October 1973.
3. House of Commons Hansard, 17 December 1973, col. 955.

12

year 7,633,000 workers had their wages cut by £4,221,500 a week; and in those two years the Ministry of Labour's index of wage rates fell by 38%. In 1972 the miners struck for increases in their deplorably low wages and won: in 1926 they had struck — for much longer — against wage *reductions* and lost. Thereafter, reductions throughout industry, though on a less drastic scale, continued up to the financial crisis of 1931 when one worker in five was unemployed, and a panic-stricken government tried to remedy the situation by cutting the salaries of civil servants, teachers and other employees. I myself, for 12 years from 1927, held a University appointment on a completely static salary without even an incremental scale. Nobody, myself included, thought this odd; but to-day my professorial successors, enjoying regular revisions, which by 1973 had raised their salaries to between six and eight times that on which I retired in 1957, would take a different view.

Quite how this method of raising ourselves by our own bootstraps came to be accepted is not altogether clear. Most of the credit must presumably go to the unions who exploited to the full both the prevailing post-war euphoria, and to the great expectations raised by the election of the first-ever Labour government to have both a comfortable majority and a zest for an ambitious programme.

Even before the war, however, the ground had been prepared at a more academic level, when in 1936 the publication of Keynes' *General Theory of Employment, Interest and Money* initiated a second revolution which turned economic theory, and in good measure economic practice also, upside down. Until the appearance of that work, uncontrollable 'trade cycles' had been accepted as facts of life no less immutable than regular wage advances subsequently became. In these recurring cycles wages, prices and the volume of employment would rise together for two or three years, after which all would come tumbling down as 'slump' succeeded 'boom', with immense consequential loss and suffering to both sides in industry, until the tide turned again and the whole process was once more repeated. Trade cycle theories were the regular stock-in-trade of every academic syllabus, while professorial lectures and treatises vied with each other in their efforts to explain how this inevitable sequence could be, if not prevented, at least predicted.

The Keynes theory was extremely complicated; but it left the old-style trade cycle stone dead. What is more, it was interpreted as throwing Victorian prudence to the winds, and as giving assurances, particularly to governments, that the need to live within their incomes was not only an old-fashioned myth, but in some circumstances positively antisocial as well. Nor did its complexities obscure the simple inference that the traditional remedy of trying to cure a slump by cutting wages was no remedy at all. To cut wages, according to Keynes, was merely to reduce the public's spending money, with the result that goods remained unsold, profits fell, industry stagnated, and more and more workers lost their jobs: in fact, far from reversing the downward trend, wage reductions merely aggravated it. Hence the way to beat a slump was for us all to go on a buying spree. I seem to remember Keynes himself giving a broadcast – in the nineteen-thirties – in which he exhorted those who were planning to buy one dress, if possible to buy two. While I doubt if many trade union leaders ploughed through the pages of *The General Theory*, therein lay a lesson that they were not slow to learn. You cannot buy two dresses instead of one, if your wages or your husband's have been cut.

A second inference that was – legitimately or illegitimately – drawn from Keynes was that, if the money in circulation is not sufficient to sustain both the public's buying power and the capacity of industry to invest in new production, this should be increased by a process known as 'reflation'. About 'reflation' I shall have something to say presently. But for the moment the essential point is that, so long as wages and other incomes were maintained, if necessary by 'reflation', there remained no visible reason why we should continue to suffer from 'trade cycles'. So a mass of economic literature on which students of my generation were brought up, was left to gather dust on library shelves, while we all looked forward to living happily ever after on perpetually rising incomes.

But, alas! there were snags. This happy sequence of rising incomes and full employment might be all right in a wholly self-sufficient domestic economy. But Britain is at all times heavily dependent on imported food and raw materials; and, to make matters worse, an increasingly affluent British public was also disposed to augment its purchases of foreign manufactures without bothering about where the exports to pay for these were coming from. Hence in the nineteen-sixties our adverse balance of payments increased at a rate which was thought to be alarming at the time (though not to be compared with what happened later). This frightened the Labour governments of the sixties into introducing a man-made substitute, known as 'stop-go', for the old-style self-perpetuating trade cycle, from the tyranny of which we thought we had so recently emancipated ourselves.

The 'stop' phase of 'stop-go', like the traditional slump, inevitably led to increasing unemployment. However, in conjunction with the devaluation of the £ and a statutory prices and incomes policy, it did at least enable the Labour government to restore a favourable balance of payments before their demise in 1970. But there was one vital difference between old-fashioned cycle and new style 'stop-go'. All through the political and economic vicissitudes of the last years of the Labour government and the first years of their Conservative successors, wages and prices continued to move steadily upwards and so, also, (and at an accelerating rate) did unemployment, which stood at over 900,000 in Great Britain throughout the first quarter of 1972. This was something new – something not in the book. According to the traditional rules, rising unemployment should coincide not with *rising*, but with *falling*, prices and wages. Clearly somebody had succeeded in changing the rules.

New rules, new policies – and new words. Two words suddenly came into fashion – namely 'reflation' and 'growth'. 'Reflation' was to be a cure for unemployment, so the Conservative Chancellor of the Exchequer's first budget was to be 'reflationary', while 'growth' would cure inflation and make possible the continued rise in living standards which was every Englishman's birthright.

Both these terms seem to have been a cover for muddled thinking. I myself remember the word 'reflation' coming into use in the 1930's in the depths of a classical-type slump, when prices, wages and salaries had for some years all been falling rapidly, with unemployment rising to unprecedented levels. We were in fact suffering from a period of severe deflation; and according to the orthodoxy of the time, the cure for deflation is inflation: trends must be reversed and money injected into the economy in order to stimulate consumer demand. Inflation, however, was already a dirty word. The early nineteen-thirties were not so far away from the inflation that followed the first world war for people to have forgotten its horrors. So 'inflation' was re-christened 'reflation' with an implication that a reflationary policy was merely a reversal of deflation involving the return to some undefined *status quo*.

16

That is my personal memory; and it is confirmed, I see, by the Oxford English Dictionary which dates the word 'reflation' to 1932 and defines it as: 'inflation undertaken after a period of deflation to restore the previous position'. If, however, that is what reflation means, it was a totally unsuitable remedy to be applied to the 1971-2 situation, since this was most conspicuously *not* the immediate successor to a 'period of deflation'. Politely disguised as a clean synonym for the dirty word 'inflation', reflation might, on Keynsian principles, have been an appropriate remedy for a classical slump in which prices and wages were falling, while unemployment was rising. But when the Chancellor came to present his 1971 and 1972 budgets there *was* no classical slump. Prices and wages, far from conforming to any classical model, were still climbing ruthlessly upwards, and continued to do so after those budgets had handed out large tax reductions, particularly to the richer taxpayers. Demonstrably the homoeopathic experiment of curing inflation by inflation had no success.

The word reflation was therefore quietly expunged from the vocabulary, and its place taken by 'growth'. Undaunted, the Conservative Government went in for a policy of 'growth' in a big way, and the tax reductions of 1971 and 1972 were supposedly justified on the ground of their growth-producing potential. Not all beneficiaries, it was hoped, would spend these bonuses solely on their personal consumption. Business men and companies were expected to reward the Chancellor's generosity by expanding their production and establishing new enterprises. Then the resulting growth of output would provide the wherewithal to meet any increased consumer demand, and everything in the garden would be lovely.

These hopes were not, however, realised. In 1971

manufacturers' capital spending on new plant and equipment was some 8% lower than in the previous year.[1] Apparently the public just let the Chancellor down. Instead of investing their money in new productive enterprises, they poured it into Stock Exchange and property speculation, with the result that share prices paradoxically reached an all-time high at a time when employment and industrial growth were in the doldrums. The Stock Exchange booms of 1971 and 1972 had little to do with the expected profits of the companies concerned, or with 'growth' in the sense of the production of real commodities such as cheese or shoes. Even if forecasts of profit and dividends played some part as between one company and another, the dramatic rise in the *Financial Times* index of share prices from 305.3 in March 1971 to an all-time high of 543.6 in May 1972 is explicable only in terms of purely speculative buying. A gigantic gambling spree was afoot. Speculator A would buy shares for £100 to-day, selling them for £120 to B to-morrow, who in turn would sell next day to C for £140. The actual certificates bought and sold might as well have been red and blue counters like tiddly winks, for all the difference that their purchase and sale made to any economic realities. Transferring pieces of paper at continually enhanced prices never made one blade of grass grow where none grew before, or one extra nut or bolt come off the assembly line.

Much the same tale has to be told of the enormous inflation of property values. Another flood of money swamped that area also, with the result that, in face of a grievous shortage of accommodation, house prices rocketed. Theoretically the building industry should have reacted by running up new houses at high speed in order to cash in on the boom. But, even apart from the dilatory methods of a not conspicu-

1. *The Times*, 14 March 1972.

ously efficient industry, planning consents would have had to be wrested either from local authorities or from a not less dilatory Government Department. Moreover, much of the price of houses is due to the cost of land; and, although in April 1972 the Government announced plans to make more land available for building, these could only have matured over a considerable period and on a limited scale. Nor has anything much been heard of them since.

Most perverse of all, however, were some of the more thrifty recipients of the Chancellor's generosity, who simply lent his bonus back to him. In April 1972 Sir Robert Bellinger, Chairman of the National Savings Committee, quoted figures to show that in the 12 months ended 31st March of that year investment in National Savings had increased by a record figure of £735 million; and that in the preceding two years a net total of £1073 million of new money had been attracted to these funds, 'whereas it had taken about eight years to add the previous £1,000 million'.[1] Nor does it seem likely that much of this money found its way into new industrial investment. Contributors to National Savings (as officially so-called) include a substantial proportion of people of modest means who save only to meet the gas bill, the rates or the season ticket renewal. Such saving neither stimulates consumer demand (as do the thriftless when they forget about the gas bill and the rates, and buy washing machines on the never-never system instead); nor does it contribute to growth.

The trouble was, in fact, that business men, who alone in a capitalist economy can initiate growth, had lost heart or — if you prefer so to put it — had turned sulky. Like striking wage-earners they failed to perform the function which the system expects of them, and indeed on which it relies for its own

1. *The Times,* 21 April 1972.

functioning; and in both cases the failure was due to the prospect of inadequate rewards. However, the captains of industry were not denounced or told to accept gratefully whatever they could get instead of making exorbitant demands. Instead, efforts were made to cajole or to lure them by financial incentives into bestirring themselves in fresh pastures.

Eventually the climate changed, and in the three months prior to the wage and price freeze of November 1972 production and investment began to pick up. Output was estimated to be increasing at the rate of 6.8% per annum[1], while unemployment gradually declined. In both business and government circles a mood of considerable euphoria was induced. The business world, which had viewed with some dismay the prospect of a Conservative government's conversion to statutory price and profit control, concluded that they would gain more on the swings of a wage freeze than they would lose on any merry-go-round of possible price control. Ministers in their turn sang paeans in praise of growth, and even the TUC joined enthusiastically in the chorus.

After all, on the face of it growth, interpreted as increased production of desirable goods and services, is an almost platitudinously desirable objective. The anti-growth school, whose adherents deplore our slavish addiction to material wealth, speak only for the comfortable middle classes. Let them confine their objections to the production of electric toothbrushes and such like superfluities! It will be time enough to listen to more far-reaching protests when everybody in the country enjoys a middle-class standard of living. Nor should we be frightened by their bogey that the only alternative to chronic unemployment is to adapt ourselves to, say, a 30-hour working week and retirement at age 50 if not before. In the 20 years to 1970 actual working hours

1. *The Times,* 15 December 1972.

fell only from 47 to just under 46 a week, and at this rate it would take over 300 years to reach a 30-hour week. At least up till now every reduction in normal working hours has merely opened the door to increased overtime, since for the great majority a higher standard of living still matters more than increased leisure. When everybody has enough of everything — (and even a drastic redistribution of existing wealth would not abolish poverty) — then, and only then, will it be time to talk of excessive growth.

It all sounds (and in principle is) simple common-sense. Growth cannot fail to be advantageous when it stands for wealth created by brains, skill, sweat and machinery. But trouble starts when the word is extended to cover the easy credit at home and abroad which is supposed to facilitate the production of goods and services. Then the line between financial and physical growth becomes blurred, critical voices are once again heard, and past experience recalled. What about the balance of payments and the parlous state of the £ on the foreign exchange markets?

Nevertheless the Conservative Government did learn some lessons from their predecessors. They learned that you cannot frighten the great British public with even the most alarming figures about an adverse balance of payments. These figures may be regularly shown on the television screen, but, so long as wages keep on rising, they have no meaning except to the sophisticated. Moreover the situation is still further obfuscated by the experts' irritating habit of expressing themselves in metaphors. What can the risk of the economy becoming 'overheated' convey to the man in the street? Nor are warnings that the end of the road would be 'national bankruptcy' any more effective. Who ever heard of a whole nation literally going bankrupt? In what court would the proceedings be heard? As to the value of the £, Harold Wilson had appeared with a long face on television in 1967 to announce the devaluation of the £ as a grave but unavoidable decision, reached only after prolonged and anxious consideration. But the Conservatives, wise after these events, resolutely turned a blind eye to the unfavourable trend in the balance of payments; and after having warned the voters during the 1970 electoral campaign that the return of a Labour government would mean another disastrous devaluation, they achieved exactly the same result with no fuss at all by allowing the £ to 'float' — which by a curious use of language, proved to be a synonym for 'sink'.

But there was one spectre which no linguistic tricks or any other jugglery could exorcise — the spectre of inflation. As the years went by it became all too plain that the government's 'counter-inflation policy' did not counter inflation. What it did achieve was to challenge yet another of our traditional orthodoxies by imposing rigid limits upon the freedom of collective bargaining; and to the unions as well as in circles far beyond their membership this freedom ranks, along with freedom of speech or the right to vote, as one of the basic democratic liberties.

Personally I have never been able to understand this conception of democracy. Collective bargains are certainly 'democratic' in the sense that they are commonly made between trade union leaders, who are elected by their members, and employers, who also have a responsibility to their fellow industrialists. Nor can this procedure be dismissed as undemocratic on the ground that the members are insufficiently consulted and that serious decisions, such as calling a strike, can be made by a narrow majority of a small executive committee. For that, after all, is equally true of Parliamentary democracy, where the consequences may be even graver. A handful of Cabinet Ministers with the support of a few hundred members of Parliament can sentence thousands of their countrymen to death by a declaration of war.

The real issue in collective bargaining is not the relation between the parties at the bargaining table and the rank and file whom they represent. The real issue lies between those parties and others who traditionally have no place or voice at the bargaining table at all, but may nevertheless be deeply concerned in what goes on·there. From the point of view of these outsiders, collective bargaining too often appears as a system of smash and grab in which they are the helpless victims. And smash and grab is not, in other contexts, a practice that commands general admiration. Freedom to break into your neighbour's house and help yourself to his property is not one of the democratic rights cherished by a free society: on the contrary it is a crime. Yet employers and employed can, and sometimes do, strike bargains which rob their neighbours just as effectively. When an agreement is reached it is they who fix the wages and we (as well as they) who pay the prices: when no bargain is struck, and industrial action follows we (as well as they) suffer loss and inconvenience.

Higher wages are not, of course, the only significant factor in the rise of prices, as union leaders, fairly enough, are the first to remind us. But since they have themselves argued with the Government as to whether the proportion of the total national product absorbed by the wage and salary bill is 61% or 62%, they can hardly deny that overall wages and salaries are a major element at least in domestic costs.[1] How large that element may be in any individual case varies from one industry to another. Thus it is the miners' misfortune, not their fault, that wage costs are particularly high in mining (though not as high as before recent increases in mechanisation).

1. TUC Report on The Chequers and Downing Street Talks, July to November 1972.

Wage increases to miners therefore come through to consumers (or to taxpayers if financed by government subsidies) with an inevitability not paralleled in, for example, the case of workers engaged in the production of electrical power. Miners moreover are doubly ill-placed because for them, as for all employees in the public service or in nationalized industries, there is never a margin of profit from which, instead of from the pockets of the consuming public or the taxpayer, their wages might be raised. But these differences, while they may significantly influence the course of negotiations, in no way affect the public's claim that he who ultimately pays even part of the piper's wage has a right to be at least consulted about the tune.

Resistance to the conception of a 'public interest', distinct from that of either employers or employed, is still very strong in union circles. In 1971, at a time when the Treasury was urging a 'progressive reduction' in pay settlements, a Court of Inquiry under Lord Wilberforce, appointed to report on a dispute in the Electricity Supply Industry, was enjoined by its terms of reference not only to examine the unions' wage claim, but also to take into account 'the industry's productivity record and the interests of the public and of the national economy'.[1] To this formula the unions concerned immediately took exception, although they were presently persuaded to withdraw their ban on overtime and policy of non-co-operation 'as an act of good faith with the nation'. In its eventual Report, however, the Tribunal was constrained to skate very delicately over this issue of 'the public interest'. Having loftily proclaimed that it would in any case have had in mind the public interest in the efficiency and viability of so important an industry, it was equally emphatic that it was not its business to 'decide between alternative

1. Cmnd 4594 of February 1971.

policies of macro-economic character'; and that staff in the electricity industry could not 'be expected to accept settlements on the lines of previous years unless there is moderation also in other pay settlements, a slower rise in prices, and some prospects of growth in their real earnings'. One member also appended a note emphasising that it 'would be contrary to the public interest' if workers in an industry with such an outstanding record of productivity 'were to be kept behind average wage levels elsewhere'. It is, however, significant that when, a year later, Lord Wilberforce was called upon to give a repeat performance in relation to the miners' dispute, no mention of the public interest was made in the terms of reference of this Tribunal, who were instructed merely to 'inquire into the causes and circumstances of the present dispute between the Coal Board and the National Union of Mineworkers over the pay and conditions of the Union's members'.[1]

Perhaps the most extreme denial of the existence of any third-party public interest in collective bargaining (or its failures) came from Vic Feather towards the end of his service as secretary of the Trades Union Congress (hereafter referred to as the TUC), when during the 1972 railway go-slow he actually went so far as to identify the unions with the public. 'We are not only representative of the public interest', he is reported to have said; 'we are the public interest.'[2] If by this he meant that 10 million unionists are a sizable proportion of an electorate of nearly 40 million, the statement is unexceptionable. But any implication that the action of the few thousand engine drivers involved in the dispute was in no way injurious either to any of the rest of their 10 million fellow unionists, or to the remaining 30

1. Cmnd 4903 of February 1972.
2. *The Times*, 17 April 1972.

million voters and their dependants, is plainly ridiculous. Every 'public' comprises a complex network of conflicting interests, and membership of an organisation cannot guarantee complete immunity from any damage arising from action by other members of the same organisation. No doubt many of the 10 million unionists cheerfully bore the inconvenience (and sometimes even financial loss) arising from the disruption of railway services, because they were sympathetic to the railwaymen's demands: and many members of the non-union public may have been equally sympathetic in this case and probably even more so in the 1972 miners' strike: but this does not obliterate the reality of the inconvenience and possible loss incurred, nor the fact that this was not confined to sympathisers.

It does indeed seem strange that in as highly régulated a society as that in which we now live, the incomes of the great majority of citizens should be settled by smash and grab between persons immediately concerned, and without reference to any one else who may be potentially affected – strange indeed, that in a world in which one cannot put up a garage in one's own garden or add a wing to one's house without planning permission, authority should abdicate when it comes to the decision as to what people ought to be paid. And strangest of all perhaps is the spectacle of Labour governments (who are after all heirs to an equalitarian socialist tradition) emphatically defending against their political opponents a system of catch-as-catch-can and the devil take the hindmost.

Nevertheless, one can see how that system, indefensible as it now appears, came into being. Without the right to bargain as a group, every individual worker is a potential threat to his neighbour, and every employer can play his employees off against one another on the good old principle of divide and conquer. Exploitation thus becomes cumulative. Only by concerted trade union action can the workers bargain on an equal, or on a one to one, basis, with their employers. And the right so to combine has only been won after long and bitter struggles. In 1824 the repeal of the Combination Acts conceded the principle; but the battles for recognition in particular industries have lasted well into this century. Small wonder, therefore, that trade unionism has itself become idealised and that it still evokes powerful sentiments of devotion and admiration amongst its members. To this day it is customary to speak of the 'Trade Union Movement', a term which carries undertones of a great social crusade, rather than of the business-like organisation of particular interests in the cause of their own advancement. Among the older union leaders, now retired from active office, these emotions are particularly fervent; and not surprisingly so, since many of them have to thank their unions for escape from grinding poverty and intolerable conditions of work. Their life stories are dramatic and moving, and their personal debt to their beloved Movement is incalculable.

However, times are changing and a third revolution has quietly evolved within the ranks of trade unionism itself. The idealism is not dead: nor are low wages and exploitation a thing of the past. But trade unionism has become respectable and is indeed now integrated into the Establishment. Trade union leaders are knighted and peerages conferred upon them, and virtually every Royal Commission or similar public body must include the 'statutory Union representative' just as much as the 'statutory woman' — whether or no its business is concerned with industrial relations. Moreover the modern trade union leader is head of a large organisation, and, in consequence, while his objectives may be different, his daily routine increasingly approximates to that of the head of any other large organisation – even those in the business world. Although his salary is probably lower than that of a business executive with comparable responsibilities, it is almost certain to be substantially higher than the average earnings of his members. Often, too, his horizons are widened by the international contacts and foreign travel involved in his official duties, and his dress and style of life place him unmistakably in the middle class. He may sit on the other side of the table from the employers' representatives, but as an administrator and negotiator he understands, and even speaks, their language. Indeed one of the curious incidental side-effects of government intervention in collective bargaining since 1972 has been the appearance of a new cordiality in the attitude of trade union leaders to the employers with whom traditionally they should be locked in unremitting conflict. 'Leave us alone' the miners' leaders kept saying during the 1973-4 dispute, 'and we can perfectly well settle our differences by negotiation with the Coal Board.' It was the Government and the Pay Board, not their employers, whom they blamed for all the trouble. Indeed this love affair eventually reached such a pitch of intensity that in February 1974 we witnessed the extraordinary spectacle of, first the Coal Board, and then British Rail, begging the Pay Board to allow them to pay higher wages to their employees – surely a unique occasion in the history of industrial relations!

Another result of the growing strength of trade unionism has been a subtle change of attitude which may go some way to explain the modern coincidence of rising unemployment with rising wages. In the days when the unions were less powerful than they are now, the unemployed could sometimes creep back into work by offering to take jobs below the union rate. To-day, however, the unions have erected barriers too solid to allow many tricks of that kind;

and, with their eyes firmly set upon such of their membership as remains employed, their leaders have perhaps become blinkered as to their possible responsibility for those who are not so fortunate. They hold firmly to the doctrine that the blame for unemployment rests solely upon government, and cannot in any sense be laid at their own door.

As a result of all these developments trade unionism can no longer be said to have quite the same quality as a social 'Movement' as it had half a century ago; and the sentiments and emotions attaching to such a Movement have a somewhat hollow ring to-day. Contemporary unions, whether they speak for professional men earning several thousands a year, or railway workers fighting for wages barely above £20 a week, are the organised representatives of sectional interests, just as much as associations of tenants or landlords or Chambers of Commerce. As such they have a legitimate, indeed a necessary, function. In complex modern societies sectional interests will not get justice unless they are organised and have competent spokesmen to put their case. But that is not to say that they have any more right than anybody else to be judge and jury in their own cause. Sectional conflicts need to be resolved by equitable adjustment of all the interests concerned, and that can only be effected by appropriate machinery. It is the absence of such machinery in the industrial field which has for too long resulted in a condition of total anarchy.

Already, however, even from within the unions themselves occasional whispers impugning the sanctity of uncontrolled collective bargaining have begun to make themselves heard. At the 1973 Labour Party Conference, Tom Jackson, secretary of the Union of Post Office Workers, voiced a complaint (which was publicised on television) that it was collective bargaining which had produced the present pattern of earnings — with an obvious implied reference to the low pay of many of his own members. To this Hugh Scanlon, on behalf of the engineering workers, replied by condoling with Mr. Jackson and hinting that some part of the earnings of the well-paid should be 'drained off by taxes' to help the postal workers and other low-paid groups.

Signs of other changes of outlook, with even more radical potentialities, are also perceptible among contemporary trade unionists. Enjoying the amenities of the middle class way of life, the union official may begin to ask himself why his members should be debarred from attaining similar standards. Between the lines of the speeches of some of the more militant trade union leaders of to-day and in some of their more 'extravagant' wage claims, one senses the ground-swell of a challenge to the basic assumption which underlies the whole pattern of our wage and salary structure — that is, the assumption that the hierarchy of standards of living should roughly correspond to the Registrar-General's social hierarchy of professional, intermediate, skilled, partly skilled and unskilled occupations — the assumption, in short, which enables middle-class professional people un-blushingly to refer to the 'very high' wages of, say, Midland car workers, when they would regard an equivalent salary in their own case as wholly derisory. 'Why should the working man not have a car, a TV set, a washing machine and a good carpet on the floor?' Jack Jones of the Transport and General Workers' Union once asked in a broadcast discussion. Why not indeed? These are quite modest demands, and do not go beyond what many working men succeed in acquiring. Nevertheless the implicit challenge to established conventions is one of the most significant social phenomena of our time.

This then, in broadest outline, is the background story. It is a story of rising public expectations and of almost universal conversion to the creed that every year we should in the nature of things, be able to say we never had it so good as last year and now we have it even better. At governmental level it is a story of attempts to impose conscious control upon the hitherto self-regulating sequence of industrial expansions and contractions. In the trade unions it is a story of growing power, of a new and assured position in the community and of new challenges.

But it is also a story of living beyond our incomes in a fool's paradise: of staggering from one short-term expedient to another; and of failure to devise, for the long term, a more civilized method of regulating incomes than legalised smash and grab.

# II

# The Trend Towards Compulsion and the Labour Government's Experiment, 1966-1970

AGAINST the background described in the previous chapter the country drifted (or perhaps 'plunged' would be a better word) into a statutory incomes policy under a Labour government in the summer of 1966. Both before and after its introduction, however, this was generally regarded as a short-term emergency measure; nor had there been much systematic discussion of two major issues which are fundamental in any policy which is to be more than a temporary expedient, namely, whether it is to be voluntary or statutory; and whether it is to cover not only wages and salaries, but all incomes, whatever their source, and if so how?

Among the few exceptions in which these issues had been raised was a pamphlet by Michael Stewart and Rex Winsbury published as early as 1963.[1] This left no doubt but that any viable policy must, in the authors' view, be fully comprehensive. Excessive business profits, it was suggested, should be caught by price control operated by a body 'analogous in some ways to the present Monopolies Commission', which would have the task of investigating 'prices and profit margins which appeared to be too high'. Should this appearance be substantiated, the firm concerned would be 'required to reduce its prices on pain of state regulation or take-over'. On the other hand, so far as the unions were concerned the authors trod very gently, the first of their minimum requirements for a successful incomes policy being 'the consent of

1. Stewart, Michael, and Winsbury, Rex. *An Incomes Policy for Labour* (Fabian Tract 350, 1963.)

the Unions', although this consent was itself to be dependent upon the application of the policy to all forms of income. At the same time, it was admitted that in the last resort 'in any organisation vulnerable to the activity of a dissident minority (a state, a trade union, an incomes policy) *some degree* [italics original] of coercion or sanction is inevitable, in this case to make it at least difficult for one union (as opposed to the unions collectively) to put an end to the whole scheme'. The nature of this sanction was not, however, discussed.

The title of this pamphlet was of some significance, because it was one of the first indications of a growing acceptance of the view that an incomes policy must be what its name implies, and not just a policy for the control of wages — although in practice, as will presently appear, noticeably less consideration has been given to 'other incomes' than to wages and salaries, or to devising a policy under which all incomes from whatever source would be treated on a uniform basis. Undoubtedly it was from the problem of wage regulation that the concept of an incomes policy originated, and to this day it is control of wages which looms largest in the minds of those concerned in framing such policies.

This attitude is explicable, though not, I shall suggest, now defensible, on several grounds. First, wages and salaries constitute far the greater part of the total of personal incomes. In 1972 wages and salaries reached a total of £33,080 million, as against figures of £4,976 million for rent, dividends and interest and £4,708 million for incomes from self-employment. Second, wages constitute the single largest item in domestic industrial costs: their total of £33,080 million has to be set against a gross national product of £53,012 million. They are therefore *prima facie* likely contributors to inflation, and as such exceptionally vulnerable. Third, changes in the level of wages affect more people than do changes in any other form of income: hence their regulation is a matter of widespread popular concern. Fourth, the control of contractual incomes (though now considerably complicated by the spread of overtime, payment by results and plant bargaining) is a relatively simple matter, since such incomes are determined by contracts (written or verbal) which can be known in advance of actual payments – whereas no one knows what his profits are till he has made (or failed to make) them. Explicit decisions, which result from bargains between employers and employees are therefore wide open to governmental interference. Even if enforcement is not always an easy matter, government can prescribe within what limits these decisions are acceptable. Finally, the fact that rates of pay are fixed after arguments which are often widely publicised means that both argument and conclusion are open to comment and criticism by anyone interested. Comparisons can readily be made between the rates paid for different jobs, with the result that violent passions are inflamed, and complex and far-reaching issues raised, by discussions of what miners, railwaymen or anyone else 'ought' to be paid.

Nevertheless that is not quite the whole story. The fact is that it is no longer *politically* possible to propound policies which restrict only incomes from employment. Even at the cost of occasional damage to intellectual integrity, it has become obligatory always to use the term 'incomes policy' even when this is merely a euphemism for a policy restricted to control of wages. No incomes policy is easy to sell, but one which frankly advocated restriction of wages alone would be totally unsalable. In 1955, when I published *The Social Foundations of Wage Policy*, that title correctly described the limited content of the book; but I was also at pains to point out[1] that I

1. on p. 185.

was dealing with only 'one item in a comprehensive social programme', that 'the best and most admirable wage policy in the world cannot . . . even guarantee "fair shares to all"', and that 'there are dangers in discussing wage policy in isolation from other measures'. In the light of later experiences those dangers now seem so formidable that I should not again venture to discuss wages policy by itself; and it is significant of the present trend that Hugh Clegg chose to use the title *'How to Run an Incomes Policy'* for a book which devotes scarcely more than two pages to 'other incomes'. Aubrey Jones likewise writing on *The New Inflation*[1] paid little attention to incomes other than wages and salaries, with the single exception of business profits; and these were discussed, not so much as a source of personal income, as in their relation to prices. But this may well be because he did not regard 'other incomes' as inflationary. A similar tendency to identify incomes policy with wage regulation and to treat profits as incidental to price control may also be observed in many of the papers contributed to a conference on incomes policy organised jointly by the Social Science Research Council and the National Institute of Economic and Social Research in 1972.[2]

Throughout the nineteen-sixties both the Conservative and the Labour governments presented at least a facade of comprehensiveness. In the words of a White Paper[3] published by the Conservative government in February 1962, 'The objective must be to keep the rate of increase of incomes within the long-term growth of national production. . . . In recent years national production per head has risen by about 2 to 2½% per year. . . . It is accordingly necessary that the

1. *The New Inflation* (Penguin Books, 1973).
2. Blackaby, Frank (ed.). *An Incomes Policy for Britain* (Heinemann Educational Books, 1972).
3. Cmnd 1626 of 1962, (italics mine, B.W.).

increase of wages and salaries, *as of other incomes,* should be kept within this figure during the next phase'. After some more detailed discussion of the criteria applicable to wage and salary claims, a further paragraph, under the heading 'Profits and Dividends' unequivocally asserted that 'Continued restraint in profits and dividends is a necessary corollary of the incomes policy outlined above', and quoted the Chancellor of the Exchequer's declaration in the House of Commons on 18 December 1961 that 'as a part of the incomes policy, appropriate corrective action would have to be taken if aggregate profits showed signs of increasing excessively as compared with wages and salaries'. Again in November 1962, another White Paper[1] which settled the details relating to an (as it turned out short-lived) National Incomes Commission repeated the government's 'pledge that if any undue growth in the aggregate of profits should result from restraint in earned incomes that growth would itself be restrained by fiscal or other appropriate means', and instructed the Commission to 'report from time to time on the need, if any, for such action to be taken'. However, after producing five reports in the next three years, the Commission sank without trace.

In its first years of office, the Labour government followed much the same line and even used much the same language as its predecessors. An initial 'Joint Statement of Intent' written in a flamboyant style characteristic of George Brown, the Minister responsible, and printed on an unusually large single sheet (which must have caused filing problems in thousands of offices) was published in December 1964, and signed by leaders of trade union and industrial organisations as well as by four Ministers. In this the government, following almost to the letter their Conservative predecessors, promised 'to use their

1. Cmnd 1844 of 1962.

fiscal powers or other appropriate means to correct any excessive growth in aggregate profits as compared with the growth of total wages and salaries, after allowing for short-term fluctuations'.

During the period of 'voluntary co-operation' which lasted until the summer of 1966 companies were therefore asked to restrict their dividends, and in general they did so. But in the torrential flow of White Papers which preceded and followed the Labour government's eventual surrender to statutory control, plans for the control of 'other incomes' had only a subsidiary, and in some cases an ill-defined, place. For example in February 1965[1] a Paper outlining the constitution and functions of the Prices and Incomes Board merely contemplated that the Board would 'keep under review the general movement of money incomes of all kinds' and 'would be able to investigate *where appropriate*[2], cases of increases in money incomes other than wages and salaries'.

In April 1965 the next Paper[3] devoted a whole paragraph to 'Other Incomes', but this amounted to little in the way of concrete proposals. Incomes of self-employed persons were said to be 'an important category of personal incomes' which 'differ from those of employees in some respects . . . Nevertheless, those who are responsible for determining or are capable of influencing the incomes of self-employed persons should be guided by the considerations relating to the settlement of incomes and, where appropriate, to the criteria for price behaviour'. In relation to the incomes of farmers and landlords, the language used was equally obscure. These were 'to a considerable extent determined by Government policy', and accordingly the government promised to

1. Cmnd 2577 of 1965.
2. my italics (B.W.)
3. Cmnd 2639 of 1965.

'have regard to the fact that increases in incomes of this type have an effect on the prices of goods and services'; and the promise to use fiscal or other powers to correct excessive growth in profits was repeated from the 1964 Statement of Intent.

By this time the end of voluntaryism was already near, and in November 1965 its death knell was sounded in yet another White Paper[1] outlining the 'early warning system' under which government would require advance notification about wage claims, negotiations and settlements. In this, however, little attention was again paid to 'other incomes', apart from a general statement that the 'overall increase in wages, salaries and other forms of incomes should be kept in line with the growth of real national output'. Then in July 1966 came the announcement[2] of an imminent standstill on prices and incomes generally, including all company distributions and dividends, accompanied by yet another repetition of the government's pledge, now rapidly becoming a ritual chant, to use fiscal or other powers to prevent any growth of excess profits. Immediately afterwards, the 1966 Prices and Incomes Act giving effect to these restrictions was passed by Parliament.

Compulsion had arrived at last. But it was intended from the outset to be on only a temporary basis. The three statutes in which it was embodied — the Prices and Incomes Acts of 1966, 1967 and 1968 — all bear the stamp of emergency legislation and were all subject to a terminal date. (Incidentally, they deserve to rank as three of the most confusing and unreadable measures which have defaced the Statute Book in recent years.) In the first instance an absolute standstill was imposed on all increases of pay together with severe restrictions on prices (but no mention of dividends) under Pt. IV of the 1966 Act, and the

1. Cmnd 2808 of 1965.
2. Cmnd 3073 of 1966.

38

duration of the relevant sections was limited to 12 months with no provision for renewal. By November, however, the end of this freeze was already in sight, heralded by yet another White Paper[1] proposing that as from 1st January 1967 the ice should melt into a 'period of severe restraint' and repeating for the fifth time the formula about the use of fiscal and other powers to control excessive profits.

Under Part I of the 1966 Act, the Prices and Incomes Board (hereafter referred to as the PIB), which had been examining questions of pay and prices on government references ever since the spring of 1965, acquired statutory status. Although the provisions governing its functions were originally restricted to a twelve months' validity, the Board itself had the unique distinction of being exempt from the statutory death sentence that hung over all the other provisions of the Act. It might, therefore, have been expected to develop into a permanent institution. But as things turned out it was destined to early execution by the Conservative government of 1970. Nevertheless during its four years of statutory life, the Board, with a membership drawn from time to time from trade unionists, representatives of the business world and academic economists (but no MPs or civil servants) remained wholly independent, and produced a uniquely valuable volume of case studies of pay and practices in a wide range of British industry and services – limited only by the fact that these investigations were restricted to matters referred by the Secretary of State.

These references could include 'any questions relating to wages, salaries or other forms of income', or to the prices charged for transactions of any description, and the Secretary of State could also require the Board in more general terms to keep such matters 'under continuous review'. In the case of

1. Cmnd 3150 of 1966.

specific references, the Act provided that no proposed wage or price increases could come into effect until the Board's Report was published, although, alternatively, the Secretary of State could himself impose a deferment of up to 30 days without reference to the Board. Provision was also made to bring dividends under control, at least to the extent that any company could be required to notify any proposed increase in its dividend rate, in order that the Secretary of State might, if he so decided, refer this to the Board. In practice, however, although many of the PIB Reports dealt in considerable detail with the profits made by various firms and industries, the Board was not specifically asked to report on any proposals relating to dividends as such.

Although, as already mentioned, the PIB had no control over its own agenda, the 1966 Act did lay down explicit instructions as to the criteria which should govern its decisions as to pay and prices. Those relating to pay, in particular, were much more lucid and realistic than anything that we have had since, and, inasmuch as they will undoubtedly provide at least a point of departure for the draft of any future statutory incomes policy, they deserve to be quoted in full. They required the PIB to work to a norm estimated to represent 'the average rate of annual increase of money incomes per head' which would be 'consistent with stability in the general level of prices', and set in the first instance at 3-3½%. Exceptional increases in pay above the norm could however be approved under the following conditions:

(i) Where the employees concerned, for example by accepting more exacting work or a major change in working practices, make a direct contribution towards increasing productivity in the particular firm or industry. Even in such cases some of the benefit should accrue to the community as a whole in the form of lower prices;

(*ii*) Where it is essential in the national interest to secure a change in the distribution of manpower (or to prevent a change which would otherwise take place) and a pay increase would be both necessary and effective for this purpose;

(*iii*) Where there is general recognition that existing wage and salary levels are too low to maintain a reasonable standard of living;

(*iv*) Where there is widespread recognition that the pay of a certain group of workers has fallen seriously out of line with the level of remuneration for similar work and needs in the national interest to be improved.

In the case of incomes other than wages, the obscure provisions of the April 1965 White Paper already quoted were also written into the 1966 Act, along with a general statement that 'It is necessary not only to create the conditions in which essential structural readjustments can be carried out smoothly but also to promote social justice'.

Working with admirable speed and efficiency in the application of these rules to such diverse subjects as the pay of higher civil servants or the remuneration of milk distributors, the PIB was kept busy by government references right down to the end of 1969. Moreover in 1967 and again 1968 its status was upgraded by new legislation, inspired less perhaps by admiration for its work than by the anxiety and gloom engendered by devaluation and the post-devaluation economic situation. In 1967 a second Prices and Incomes Act extended the period of deferment in cases on which the Board reported adversely. The relevant sections of this statute are more than a little complicated, but the upshot was that applications for increases in prices or pay could be forbidden to take effect for a maximum of six months from the date of reference to the Board; and in the third and final Act of 1968 these six months were still further extended to twelve, while a new provision gave the Treasury power itself to prohibit companies from declaring dividends at a higher rate than that paid in the preceding year.

The 1968 Act, the last of the trio, was due in its turn to expire at the end of 1969. But by then the tide had turned and the power of deferment was once more restricted, as in 1966, to one month during examination of claims by the Secretary of State, or, if referred by him to the PIB, to a further three months pending publication of its Report. Finally, after the Conservative government took office in June 1970, no further applications were referred to the Board, and at the end of March 1971, when all the cases in hand had been dealt with, it was compelled to put up its shutters, bequeathing to — one hopes an appreciative — posterity its 170 Reports.

Every item but one of this patchwork legislation was thus under sentence of death from the day that it was enacted, while the one exception — the PIB itself — perished shortly after the rest.

As might be expected in a policy designed for so short a life, no new or comprehensive criterion of equity was formulated. The prescribed norm involved acceptance of the existing structure, subject only to the specific exceptions provided in the rubric governing the operations of the PIB, and to the pious reference to social justice in the White Paper of April 1965, repeated in the 1966 Act. Moreover, although these exceptions included cases where there was 'general recognition' that wages were too low to maintain a reasonable standard of living, or where there was 'widespread recognition' that the pay of certain workers had fallen seriously out of line with that of others doing similar work, in neither case was any survey undertaken to establish either what was generally regarded as a reasonable standard of living, or which workers were 'widely recognised' as having fallen seriously out of line with others whose work might be regarded as similar. The PIB did indeed produce one Report on *The General Problems of Low Pay* (No.169), in response to a government direction to investigate the pay of ancillary workers in the National Health Service, workers in the laundry and dry cleaning industry and in contract cleaning. In this Report the low-paid were defined as those whose 'earnings fall into the bottom tenth of the "earnings league"',' although the Board was aware that such a definition 'could be criticised on the grounds that there will always be a bottom tenth, so that the problem is insoluble'; and in this, as also in other Reports dealing with particular cases, the Board clearly appreciated that preferential treatment to the low-paid must inevitably disturb relativities. But, as the Board itself emphasised, its terms of reference on this particular topic necessarily limited the scope of its conclusions, which were indeed obvious rather than profound; and it is perhaps significant that this Report was the last but one in the whole series, and appeared on the eve of the Board's own demise.

As to the 'comparability' criterion in a wider sense, Professor Clegg (himself a full-time member of the Board for the first eighteen months of its life) has remarked that the Board was 'almost as frightened of this standard as were the Government'.[1] However, in practice, the PIB, while disclaiming 'any absolute opposition to the use of comparisons in wage determination',[2] did show considerable determination throughout its work (notably in its Reports on Railways Pay (No.8) and on Pay of the Industrial Civil Service (No.18)) to give less weight to these than had hitherto been customary.

1. Clegg, Professor Hugh. *How to Run an Incomes Policy* (Heinemann Educational Books, 1971) p.20.
2. Fels, Allan. *The British Prices and Incomes Board* (Cambridge University Press, 1972) p.109.

Hard feelings were nevertheless provoked by inequalities arising from failure to give sufficient attention to the discrepancy between wage rates as nationally or regionally negotiated and actual earn-- ings, which had been growing rapidly since the war. In some industries as much as half — and even occasionally more than half — of a worker's pay packet may be made up of overtime payments, bonuses and a multiplicity of special rates which are settled by bargaining on the shop floor, the details of which are not known outside the plants in which they operate, and are much too complicated to be covered by any general wage agreement. Nor can these be safely regarded as non-inflationary on the ground that they are the rewards of extra productivity. The plain truth is that much overtime and a great variety of 'plus rates', shift allowances and the like, are simply means of getting extra money in return for very dubious increases in production. These extras, more-over, are very unevenly dispersed amongst the whole wage and salary-earning community. Thousands of salaried workers are paid by rates strictly fixed in advance and have no opportunity of increasing their earnings either by overtime or by other ingenious devices. For the mass of salary earners a standstill is therefore literally a standstill — even if in some professions, such as university teaching, there may be opportunities for pickings on the side. The Labour government's experiment effectively demonstrated that any future statutory policy must, if it is to be genuinely non-inflationary, find a way of controlling pay that takes account of actual earnings, and not merely of basic rates.

On the general principle of comparability the Board never produced one of its special reports, but brief discussions of the issues involved were occasion-ally included in the General Reports published at intervals. In the first of these (No.19 of August,

1966, p.16), the Board observed that 'The social case for special treatment for particular groups of workers who have fallen behind in pay has led to the multiplication of . . . formulas' which 'are open to the criticisms that the choice of some of the comparisons is not easily justified', and that these formulas '. . . provide a mechanism for spreading increases in wage rates from one group to another, regardless of the reasons for which the original increases were given. . . . What began as a means of providing special treatment where there was a special case for it has tended, . . . to become a device for spreading through the economy increases in wage rates originating in the needs of particular industries'. In consequence 'the doctrine of comparisons' could actually 'frustrate the social case for special treatment for particular groups'. It was therefore recommended that these formulas should be no longer used.

Three years later, in its fourth General Report (No.122 of 1969, p.23) the PIB reverted to the subject. After repeating the substance of the previous argument quoted above, this Report concluded that 'the concept of comparability has clear dangers'. Not only was it highly inflationary, but its invocation also tended 'to drive out of sight factors of greater importance, such as the need to adjust the structure of earnings internally . . . or the need to found an increase in pay on greater efficiency'; and after the Board's demise Joan Mitchell, one of its part-time members from 1965-68, even went so far as to refer to 'the obnoxious principle' of comparability.[1]

In its attitude towards the productivity criterion, the Board was again decidedly critical. Although this rubric was already drafted in fairly stiff terms, the Board nevertheless concluded that the safeguards should be drawn even more tightly. In its General

---

1. Mitchell, J. *The National Board for Prices and Incomes* (Secker & Warburg, 1972), p.196.

Report on Productivity Agreements (No.36) it therefore proposed to re-write the guide lines as follows:

(*i*) It should be shown that the workers are making a
direct contribution towards increasing productivity by
accepting more exacting work or a major change in
working practices.

(*ii*) Forecasts of increased productivity should be derived
by the application of proper work-standards.

(*iii*) An accurate calculation of the gains and the costs
should normally show that the total cost per unit of
output, taking into account the effect on capital, will
be reduced.

(*iv*) The scheme should contain effective controls to ensure
that the projected increase in productivity is achieved,
and that payment is made only as productivity
increases or as changes in working practice take place.

(*v*) The undertaking should be ready to show clear
benefits to the consumer through a contribution to
stable prices.

(*vi*) An agreement covering part of an undertaking should
bear the cost of consequential increases elsewhere in
the same undertaking, if any have to be granted.

(*vii*) In all cases negotiators should beware of setting
extravagant levels of pay which would provoke resentment outside.

Not many cases, one would imagine, would manage
to pass all these hurdles.

Equally lacking in cordiality was the PIB's attitude
to the exceptional treatment of cases in which the
distribution of manpower might be influenced in the
national interest. On this issue it took the line that in
areas with a general manpower scarcity labour shortages were unlikely to be remedied by exceptional
increases in pay, unless those increases were very
large. This doctrine is said to have been applied 'in
reference after reference, with few exceptions, and
investigations in particular cases were designed to

show the futility of overcoming labour shortages by means of pay increases'.[1] Thus the *Report on the Pay and Conditions of Busmen* (No.16) enunciated the principle that 'The most effective remedy for an undertaking suffering from a shortage of labour' in an area of general manpower shortage is 'to make better use of the labour which it already has;' and to this end London Transport was advised 'not to man an establishment based on a historical pattern of services, but to secure a continuous adaptation of manning and staffing practices to changing techniques and requirements'. Apart from the obvious merit of this advice in itself, it is certainly true, that of all the claims for exceptional increases permitted by the 1966 Act, the most difficult to justify convincingly were those based on the ground that a redistribution of manpower was necessary in the national interest, and that an increase in pay could be relied on to effect this. Figures can be produced to establish whether a wage will or will not provide an acceptable standard of living, or to show how the pay of one group of workers compares with that of another; but to rank various industries in terms of their national importance, and thereafter to determine the effectiveness of pay increases upon the distribution of manpower involves reliance upon hypothetical assumptions rather than upon objective fact. All in all, it is perhaps a fair summary to say that, while the PIB was on principle chary of allowing exceptions under the comparability criteria, its cool attitude to claims on grounds of maldistribution of labour was simply due to the necessity of keeping within the bounds of the practicable.

On a wider front the 1966-70 experiment is also open to criticism inasmuch as it failed to deal with every type of income on the same basis. While it was in name a 'Prices and Incomes Policy', in substance it

1. Fels, *op.cit.* p.106.

gave overwhelming predominance to control of prices and wages. Considerable trouble had obviously been taken to make the provisions relating to prices *appear* to be closely parallel to those which referred to wages. But there was no direct control of business incomes as such, and company dividends were not subject throughout to the same provisions as pay and prices. Dividends were not even mentioned in Part IV of the 1966 Act, which instituted the temporary standstill; and not until the 1968 Act was the Treasury expressly authorized itself to impose any restriction on them.

In any case, the analogy between restrictions on wages and on dividends has only superficial validity. A company which makes substantial profits but is prevented (either by law or by agreement) from distributing these to its shareholders can tuck the surplus away into reserves from which, if and when restrictions are lifted, future dividends can be swollen, or bonus shares distributed. But the wage increases that a worker forgoes to-day are not similarly saved up for his subsequent enjoyment. Again, company shareholders are a miscellaneous collection in a sense which does not apply equally to miners or railwaymen. The shareholders in any company may be millionaires or impoverished widows and orphans, (the latter apparently predominating when there is any question of taxation or dividend limitation) or anything in between. They may be idle or industrious, active or retired. About their personal circumstances their directors do not know, and have no right to know, anything. Railwaymen on the other hand are all engaged in work on railways, and miners work in and about the mines. While some of them may have other resources beside their wages, and one or two here and there may be lucky enough to have won substantial dividends on the pools, their employers, as well as any members of the public sufficiently interested, can get a reasonably clear picture of their normal personal earnings; and the same is true of other wage-earning or salaried groups, all of whom are thus in a totally different position from the miscellaneous body of shareholders.

The method of dealing with both joint-stock dividends and business profits generally under the 1966-8 Acts in fact established an important but unfortunate precedent, which has been followed in later legislation. The PIB Reports were concerned either with the pay of employed persons, or with the prices charged for goods. The Board was not specifically asked to investigate whether the profits made in a particular industry were excessive, but only whether the level of profits was an indication that the prices charged were unduly high. Many of its reports on prices did indeed discuss costs and margins in this context, but profits came into the picture only as related to prices, rather than as evidence of the personal income of individuals. Only in a few cases, notably architects and solicitors, did the Board inquire into the incomes which certain independent professional practitioners realised from the fees which they charged. Thus an incomes policy as then (and subsequently) understood, regulated wages in a way that made it possible to trace back its effect on individuals, whereas the mechanism for controlling profits and dividends was such that the results upon individuals were totally unpredictable. When it comes to the broader considerations of equity involved in the design of a long-term policy, this will prove to be a point of great importance.

Finally, on its major objective of containing inflation the 1966-70 record is poor. During 1965 and the first half of 1966, when the (voluntary) norm was 3-3½%, weekly earnings were rising at about 8% a year. 'During 1967, with a zero norm, or no norm,

49

and all increases requiring exceptional justification, the increase was about 6%. In 1968 and 1969, with a ceiling of 3½%, the rate of growth returned to the 1965 level'. Quoting these figures Professor Clegg concluded that, judged merely on their evidence, 'the whole policy was a colossal failure'. For this he gives a number of detailed reasons but perhaps the root of the matter was that 'Unions (and employers) were more ready to agree to a document which offered plenty of loopholes than to a tightly-drawn set of rules; and the government was anxious above all for an *agreed* [italics original] policy'.... 'There were always to hand a number of pay increases over the norm which seemed no more justified by the national interest than one's own claim'.[1] Undoubtedly also much of the discrepancy between the norm and the reality was due to neglect, as already mentioned, of the effects of plant bargaining upon earnings.

Must then the verdict 'colossal failure' be applied to the whole experiment? That would indeed be a harsh judgment — and not, I think, justified. In spite of the restrictions upon its scope, the PIB could claim to have broken new ground in the practice of deciding wage claims within certain prescribed principles. Potentially the PIB could have been a most valuable instrument for bringing some sort of order into the chaotic picture of relative wages; and it will be argued later that, without some such body, no rational policy can be evolved in so far as incomes from employment are concerned. The Board's actual achievements were, however, greatly restricted by the fact that it was allowed no initiative in the selection of cases to be investigated. It was required to examine only those applications which the Secretary of State instructed it to examine and no others; and no discernible principle appears to have governed his choice (except for the exclusion of such classes as

1. Clegg, *op.cit.* pp.13, 14.

doctors and teachers for whom special machinery already existed). In consequence the list of the Board's Reports is curiously miscellaneous. Some dealt with the pay of whole professions or industries such as nurses and midwives in the National Health Service or agricultural workers in England and Wales, some with limited classes of employees, such as the salaried staff of Imperial Chemical Industries or the Midland Bank, others with purely local groups as for example busmen in Great Yarmouth or dockers in Bristol. In a few cases, such as that of the Armed Forces or university teachers, standing references were made so that these were the subject of successive Reports issued at intervals. Certainly no rational or coherent blueprint for the pattern of wages as a whole could have been produced from such an oddly assorted sample.

Perhaps, also, any final assessment of the whole experiment must be influenced by a doubt as to whether the authors of the 1966-8 Acts ever set much store by their effectiveness. At any rate the penalties prescribed for infringements were remarkably moderate. For most offences the maximum fine that could be imposed on summary conviction was £100, while, if convicted on indictment, corporate bodies were liable to unlimited fines, but individuals only to a maximum of £500; but for failure to report wage settlements or increases in dividends as required under the 1966 Act the maximum fine was only £50. Nor was there in any case any power of imprisonment. Prosecutions, moreover, except in the case of the temporary standstill, could only be initiated with the approval of the Attorney-General. Yet even these penalties were never inflicted upon anybody, since not one prosecution under any of the three Acts was ever undertaken. Are we therefore to infer that not one single firm ever failed to notify its intention to increase prices or pay, or to defer the operation of such increases as required by law? Can it be that the modest penalties prescribed were a one hundred per cent effective deterrent? Or must we conclude that the government had so little stomach for its own theoretically enforceable policy that it was content to leave it unenforced?

Certainly no time was lost by the progenitors of this legislation in disowning their child after its death. In the — not very lucid — interval between the end of the Labour government's statutory policy and the beginning of their successors' experiment in compulsion, the statutory-voluntary debate broke out in earnest. Amongst the academics, Hugh Clegg writing in 1971[1] went so far as to propose that all claims for increases should be reviewed by a tripartite administration representing government, employers and unions, to whose decisions 'the government will have to be prepared to give the force of law . . . so that minorities cannot profit from the general restraint by pushing unjustified claims, or by cheating'. But at the same time he emphasised that 'there are fairly narrow limits to the support which the law can give to an incomes policy. . . . It can do little for an unpopular policy'; and he gave no indication as to the actual method by which the 'force of law' should be made effective.

Amongst the Labour Party leaders, whose traditional distaste for statutory controls was in many cases actually re-vitalised by their government's temporary lapse into compulsion, a few continued to make occasional references in favourable terms to a possible voluntary policy; but these gradually became vaguer and vaguer. Although the programme submitted to the 1972 Party Conference opened with the words 'We are a democratic Socialist Party, and proud of it', and proposed to stiffen the taxation of the

1. Clegg, Hugh. *How to Run an Incomes Policy* (Heinemann Educational Books, 1971), pp.57, 58, 69.

well-to-do, its only explicit reference to an incomes policy was the statement that 'We . . . intend to supplement our strict price controls, in both the private and public sectors, with a voluntary incomes policy — the objective of which must be to ensure that the growth of the nation's wealth is accompanied by steadily rising real income, with sharper rises for the lower paid'. A few months later, however, when a 'great compact' was (as the *Times* put it) 'solemnized' between the Labour Party and the TUC in a wide-ranging joint statement on *Economic Policy and the Cost of Living,* any explicit reference to an incomes policy was studiously avoided. The statement forecast that questions of industrial efficiency would entail further extensions of collective bargaining, from national to plant level, and that 'common lines of action' would be necessary at both national and international levels; but it was also no less emphatic that 'policy in this field' could 'only be based on agreement and not on compulsion'.

To this Mr. Wilson himself is reported to have added that Labour rejected statutory wage controls on the 'simple ground that history has shown that in democratic countries you can only do this once. . . . Each time you try a statutory freeze it diminishes in value and acceptability'.[1] What the evidence for this last observation may be is far from clear. Presumably it was directed against the Conservative government's reintroduction of statutory controls in November 1972: but at the time this had not got beyond the Stage 1 temporary freeze; and examples of other democratic countries in which (war-time restrictions apart) repeated attempts to operate statutory policies have come to grief are hardly conspicuous. Possibly Mr. Wilson had in mind the Dutch, who have tried hardest and longest, (and, it is widely held, most successfully). From 1945 to 1970, the Dutch govern-

1. *The Times,* 1 March 1973.

ment[1] intervened in the bargaining process with varying degrees of authority; and their story has on the whole been one of progressive relaxation with a brief return to statutory control in 1970-71, planned to last for only one year. In the first phase regular 'rounds' of wage increases were subject to uniform restrictions. In 1959 this was followed by a more flexible 'differential' system under which attempts were made to relate increases to productivity, while in 1967 the primary responsibility for collective bargaining was restored to the contracting parties, although agreements were still subject to official surveillance, and were liable to be (and sometimes were) declared 'non-binding'; but in the summer of 1971 all legislative control of both wages and prices was revoked — only later to be replaced by a 'gentlemen's agreement' under which both sides in industry agreed that wages and prices must be so controlled that there would be no advance in real standards of living during 1973. History (with the help of the Dutch, perhaps) may yet prove the truth of Mr. Wilson's sweeping assertion, but at the time that this was made it certainly had not done so. Nevertheless in the Election campaign of February 1974, it was official Labour policy to advocate, in the terms of the Joint Statement with the TUC, 'direct statutory action on prices', coupled if necessary with food subsidies, but without any restrictions on collective bargaining; and to that policy the government then elected was committed.

During the drafting of the Party's campaign programme, however, it was rightly or wrongly hinted[2] that some members of the Shadow Cabinet, while adhering to the view that a voluntary policy was to be preferred, still felt that a Labour government would

1. For a fuller account of the Dutch experiments see Blackaby, Frank (ed.). *An Incomes Policy for Britain* (Heinemann Educational Books, 1972.)
2. *The Times,* 4 January 1974.

need to build in a 'failsafe mechanism' which would impose sanctions on those unions which broke the rules. If these dissentients existed, perhaps they were mindful of the rueful comment of a White Paper issued by their own government in December 1969[1], to the effect that 'Unfortunately there is at present little evidence that higher paid workers would not take advantage for their own purposes of the attempt to help the low paid through the establishment by law of a national minimum', by using this as 'a new base on which to rebuild their existing differentials'.

The wording of the Labour Election Manifesto of February 1974 did not, however, betray any sign that either these views, or Tom Jackson's plea that it is free collective bargaining which is responsible for the present pattern of wages, had had any significant effect on Labour policy. After outlining a comprehensive social programme and elevating the Joint Statement with the TUC into a 'social contract' with the unions, the Manifesto proceeded to claim that 'only practical action by the Government to create a much fairer distribution of the national wealth can convince the worker and his family and his trade union that an "incomes policy" [quotation marks original] is not some kind of trick to force him, particularly if he works in a public service or nationalized industry, to bear the brunt of the national burden'. As, however, a Labour government was said to be ready to act 'against high prices, rents and other impositions falling most heavily on the low-paid and on pensioners', the Party was confident that 'the trade unions voluntarily (which is the only way it can be done for any period in a free society) will co-operate to make the whole policy successful', and that the action proposed on prices, together with the understanding with the TUC, 'will create the right

1. Cmnd 4237 of 1969.

55

economic climate for money incomes to grow in line with production'.

While the Labour Party was thus steadily reverting to its original distrust of any compulsory policy, the Conservative government, which had come into power in 1970 on a manifesto pledging that there would be no repetition of Labour's lapse into compulsion, at first fully shared their predecessors' disenchantment. Some of their supporters, however, already had other views. In February 1971 the Bow Group came out with a most drastic Memorandum,[1] which not only gave uncompromising support to a statutory policy, though still regarding this as a 'regrettable necessity', but also tore away any pretence that restriction should extend to any incomes other than those of wage-earners, or indeed of a limited section of the wage-earning population. Without legislative controls, according to the spokesman of the Bow Group, it needed only 'a few groups of greedy power bargainers to set up inflationary pressures which cannot or will not be contained by monetary and fiscal policies within the context of a liberal democracy'. This policy was moreover to be enforced by sanctions so severe (and so selective) that it is hardly surprising that the Report carried the title *The Wages of Fear*. These included forfeiture of any legal increase in pay, fines upon unofficial ring-leaders, to be collected by attachment of wages, forfeiture of future redundancy payments, fining of recalcitrant unions, financial support for employers confronted by strikes in support of inflationary pay claims and levies on employers who conceded such claims. These terrors, moreover, were to hang over the heads only of parties to collective bargains. Incomes from interest and dividends were to be exempt from control on the ground that 'it is impossible to operate a capitalist

1. Nelson-Jones, John. *The Wages of Fear* (The Bow Group, 1971.)

system and at the same time impose artificial restraints on interest and dividends' (wage restriction being presumably natural, not 'artificial'); and a similar privilege was to be conferred upon 'persons who do not indulge in restrictive practices or collective action'.

At a more influential level, Mr. Maudling, writing in the *Times*,[1] also accepted the need for statutory controls as a permanent feature of contemporary capitalism, though in more moderate terms than those of the Bow Group Memorandum; and the force of his article was enhanced by the fact that, had he not resigned his office, it would have been submitted to the Cabinet. Mr. Maudling was impressed by the 'profound changes, both economical and political in the whole capitalist system', and by 'an arising consciousness of the power of organised labour', which he traced partly to the spread of education, and partly to the indispensability in complex modern industry of relatively small but organisable groups. From these developments he concluded that, while 'as much as possible should be done by voluntary agreement', 'in modern political circumstances a capitalist economy must be prepared to accept a far greater degree of systematic control over the level of incomes and prices than we have ever contemplated before'.

Next day, however, from the Labour side, Mr. Richard Crossman dismissed Mr. Maudling as being 'so wrong' mainly on the ground that 'a politician has to rely chiefly on two assets — the authority he wields and the goodwill he engenders' — and that these had been destroyed by both the Wilson and the Heath Cabinets. Wilson, according to Crossman, had thrown away trade union goodwill by his abortive Industrial Relations Bill, and had lost the 'last remnants of his authority' when he capitulated and failed to push this through; while Heath had outraged

1. *The Times*, 12 September 1972.

the unions by 'a whole series of anti-working-class mini and major budgets' and 'tried to bludgeon' them with his own Industrial Relations Act.

Faith in voluntaryism died hard, but as the months went by it began to weaken, while the Conservative government struggled in vain to keep it alive by interminable but fruitless discussions with the Confederation of British Industry (hereafter referred to as the CBI) and the TUC, until its final capitulation in the autumn of 1972, described in the Chapter that follows. Of the three main political parties, therefore, only the Liberals have remained consistently committed without reservation (at least since their 1972 and 1973 Assemblies) to a statutory policy. In the February 1974 Election campaign, the Party came out with a scheme to control both prices and wages by a tax surcharge which would seem to be in principle akin to the main proposal advanced later in this book, but apparently differs from this in important aspects of its practical operation. Little more, however, has been heard of this since the Election and details are not available at the time of writing.

By the summer of 1972 the Press was flying kites in favour of a return to statutory controls, although again this was still commonly envisaged as only a temporary emergency. In August the *Daily Telegraph*[1] expressed the editorial opinion that 'What is wanted from the Government is, in the short term, statutory restraint on wages, and for the long run, a stricter control of the money supply and some kind of fiscal action to bring about a radical increase in the profitability of industrial production'. And a few weeks later *The Sun*[2] went further with proposals for a generous minimum wage, together with a freeze on all wages, salaries, prices, dividends and rents during a 'stabilising period'. During this freeze, appeals against

1. The *Daily Telegraph*, 9 August 1972.
2. *The Sun*, 26 September 1972.

'severe anomalies' were to be dealt with by a 'modernised version' of the Prices and Incomes Board; and afterwards 'a new fair pay and prices system . . . would be established, AND BACKED BY LAW' [capitals original].

Finally Mr. Aubrey Jones has thrown the great weight of his experience as chairman of the Prices and Incomes Board behind a long-term compulsory policy. 'The case for voluntarism',[1] he writes, 'is that men are not automata; they will comply provided they see reason why they should comply'. Nevertheless, 'sanctions are widely applied against individuals when their behaviour places at risk the welfare of other individuals or of the whole society of which they are members. The objection to sanctions on prices and incomes can scarcely be based on the ground that the economic interest of the individual automatically coincides with that of society. We have seen that it does not'. Mr. Jones therefore recommended the re-establishment of a Prices and Incomes Board comparable to that over which he presided until its untimely demise. Acting in a spirit of conciliation this Board would be empowered to make independent awards in accordance with general directives prescribed by government; and in the last resort a charge of failure to observe these would be the subject of court proceedings which, in the event of the case being proved, would result in the imposition of an appropriate fine.

This surely touches the root of the matter. Men certainly do comply when they see reason why they should comply. But in the absence of compelling reason, they do not. The real weakness of a voluntary incomes policy is that it depends upon universal obedience to the commandment 'Thou shalt do what it would be a good thing for everybody else to do'; and obedience to this commandment is notoriously

1. *The New Inflation,* pp.201-203.

difficult to secure. In this respect a voluntary incomes policy is an exact parallel to a proposal for voluntary disarmament. Every nation would be only too willing to disarm if every other nation was certain to do the same: but nobody dares to be first, lest another should break the rules.

So also with incomes policy. Those who practise moderation will only reap the reward of their virtue if everyone else is equally restrained. Hence, the temptation for safety's sake to ignore the demand for restraint is likely to prove irresistible. The union which breaks the commandment to do what it would be a good thing for everybody else to do, and gets an inflationary rise for its members, scores a definite gain, so long as others do not follow suit. If they do, the gain is eroded; and the moral is as in the fable of the parishioners who decided to give their priest on his retirement a cask of wine to which they would each make a contribution, passing the cask from house to house. The first contributor said to himself that 'one litre of water would never be noticed in so large a cask' and acted accordingly. The priest received a cask of water.

# III

## Compulsion under the Conservatives: The Counter-Inflation Acts, 1972 and 1973

FOR THE first two years of their reign the Conservative government of 1970 were disposed to let things rip in their unremitting devotion to 'growth'. But by June 1972 with a sinking £ and a rising adverse balance of payments, with unemployment up by nearly 40% and retail prices by nearly 17% since the election, it was impossible any longer to live on optimism. Having promised not to repeat what they had described as the 'failure' of Labour's statutory policy, and having apparently no original ideas of their own, the government began to look abroad for possible remedies. Mr. Heath apparently, when visiting top politicians in other countries, developed a habit of picking his hosts' brains in a search for incomes policies which he could plagiarise. In September 1972 he came up with what looked like an Irish model,[1] presumably as the result of discussions with the Irish Prime Minister which must have ranged beyond the state of Ireland. This was a proposal for a flat-rate increase of pay of £2 a head, coupled with a voluntary restriction designed to keep increases in retail prices within 5% for the next twelve months. A similar arrangement, under an agreement between the Irish Federated Union of Employers and the Congress of Trade Unions had been in operation in Eire for nearly two years. At first this allowed £2 a week all round, with additions to cover substantial rises in the cost of living. Later, a series of graded percentage rates was substituted, the rates varying from a maximum of 9% for incomes up to £30 a

1. *New Society*, 5 October 1972.

week down to 4% on incomes over £40. Even at this eleventh hour Mr. Heath was still showing a remarkably robust confidence that he had carried both the CBI and the TUC into serious consideration of a voluntary counter-inflationary scheme. 'All three parties' (i.e. the government, the CBI and the TUC), he is reported to have said, 'are determined to do their utmost to maintain a voluntary system and we are going to do the job'.[1]

'Their utmost', however, proved not to be enough and the job was not done; no more was heard of the £2 a week proposal. Within two months, on 6 November 1972, the Prime Minister announced in the House of Commons that, owing to failure to reach agreement, it would be necessary to bring in statutory measures, and that, as the main legislation would take time, an interim Bill would be introduced imposing an immediate standstill on prices, rents, dividends and pay. This followed immediately, and became law on the last day of November 1972 as the Counter-Inflation (Temporary Provisions) Act.

No pretence was made that the new Act was anything more than a rush job to meet a temporary emergency. It was to remain in force for 90 days with the possibility of extension by Order in Council for a further sixty days, subject to affirmative resolution of both Houses of Parliament. For the duration of the standstill (which eventually lasted till the 31 March 1973) the appropriate Minister was to have power to prohibit all increases of pay or prices or dividends in such cases as he thought fit. In the case of pay, increases agreed and put into effect before 6 November 1972 were to be allowed; but agreements already made for increases due to take effect after that date had to be deferred until the end of the standstill. The Act was, therefore, in substance (apart from the power to control dividends) a reincarnation

1. *The Times,* 27 September 1972.

of Part IV of the Labour government's Act of 1966; and a melancholy chapter of history was thus repeated.

In the result, the freeze operated very unequally. So far as wage agreements were concerned the ice was hard-packed and no one was able to crack it. Those who had concluded agreements before November 6 were the lucky ones, but not so those who had just missed the crucial date. Naturally this created a great sense of injustice and stored up many anomalies for the future. However, earnings continued to rise, though at slightly less than half the rate of the previous six months. Between October 1972 and April 1973 the increase was 4.27% as against 8.66% in the previous half-year. But if prices were 'frozen' this must have been the hottest freeze ever recorded. The retail price index rose even faster during the freeze than it had in the previous six months: between October 1972 and April 1973 the increase was 4.7% as compared with 4.3% between April and October 1972; and, moreover, the rise was very much faster than it had been throughout the preceding eighteen months.

If the Prime Minister's first, abortive, package was borrowed from Ireland, his second model was American. But the American story, even more than the British, has been one of extempore makeshifts and of almost unbelievable reversals of policy. It began with a three months' freeze in August 1971. In October this was followed by Phase II under which a Pay Board and a Price Commission were established, the former with equal representation of labour, management and 'the public'. The Board was to control wage increases in accordance with a general 'guide-line of 5.5%' for the twelve months following the end of the temporary freeze in November 1971. In the case of companies employing over 5000 workers the Board's prior approval had to be

INCOMES POLICY: AN INQUEST AND A PROPOSAL

obtained for any increases in pay, while smaller firms were obliged only to report changes after they had been introduced. But the Board soon ran into trouble. In March 1972 three of its trade union members resigned, on the ground that 'The Administration's so-called new economic policy is heavily loaded against the worker and consumer, in favour of the profits of big business and the banks, and is dominated by the view that economic progress begins and ends in the stock market and the corporate financial report'.[1] Since at no time did the Board deal with incomes other than wages, nor indeed does it appear to have been designed to do so, this criticism would seem to have had some justification.

Nevertheless the American Phase II survived for fourteen months, not without moderate success in the control of both wages and prices. Then, in December 1972, Mr. George Schultz,[2] Secretary to the Treasury, is reported to have announced that President Nixon would presently be asking Congress to extend the mandatory wage-price controls for a further period, while a week or two later Dr. Arthur Burns,[3] Chairman of the Federal Reserve Board, was reported as having admitted (in what was described as a 'relentlessly tough speech') that 'market forces no longer can be counted on to check the upward curve of wages and prices'. But Mr. Nixon did nothing of the kind. Instead, in introducing Phase III in January 1973, just when the British government was applauding the transatlantic experiment, he abolished both Pay Board and Price Commission, and relaxed controls so that large companies no longer had to give advance notification of projected price rises, with the result that the status of the 5.5% wage guide-line became extremely obscure. However this Phase lasted

1. *The Times,* 23 March 1972.
2. *The Times,* 12 December 1972.
3. *The Times,* 30 December 1972.

64

less than six months. In June 1973 Phase IV heralded a new price freeze, this time without any control of wages, although corporations were told that the 5.5% standard still applied. Not surprisingly, these turns and counter-turns appear to have been viewed with considerable cynicism. In the *Wall Street Journal* of 25 October 1973 an unnamed economist is quoted to the effect that 'it would be nice if the controls are completely discredited before they are removed'. A few months later, discredited or not, removed they were.

These vicissitudes did not, however, deter the Heath government from copying the U.S. model with considerable faithfulness. In January 1973 a White Paper was published giving a broad outline of the government's proposals, followed by a 'Consultative Document' in February and yet another White Paper in March. While all these documents were 'maddeningly inconsistent in some points',[1] the basic provisions were not afterwards significantly modified. Then, on the 22 March 1973 the projected 'main legislation' reached the Statute Book in the shape of the Counter-Inflation Act 1973 providing for the continuance of controls on prices, pay, dividends and rent for a period of three years, and establishing the Price Commission and the Pay Board. Thus, paradoxically, a Conservative government accepted an enforceable incomes policy as at least a temporary necessity in a capitalist society, whilst a professedly socialist party had decided to leave this crucial issue permanently exposed to the hazards of voluntary agreement. But perhaps Labour opinion would not have hardened so much against all forms of statutory control had it not been for the conversion of their opponents to the contrary point of view.

It is therefore to the Americans that we owe the practice of legislating only for a few months at a time in a succession of 'Phases', or (as we have re-

1. *Incomes Data Services,* Report No. 158, April 1973.

christened them perhaps in order to demonstrate our independence) 'Stages'; and it is from the Americans that we have borrowed the dyarchy of Price Commission and Pay Board, in this case copying even the names. No convincing reasons were, however, ever given by our government for departing from the precedent of a single Prices and Incomes Board. Challenged in the Lords to produce positive arguments in support of the proposed dyarchy, Lord Jellicoe devoted much of his speech to assurances that the two bodies would work very closely together, sharing the same offices as well as certain common services and staff; and that, if circumstances should so indicate, they could be amalgamated at a later date. In his search for positive arguments the best he could do was to emphasise that, unlike the Prices and Incomes Board, the new agencies would have executive as well as advisory powers, and that it would be imperative for them to be able to make 'clean, quick decisions'.[1] Yet it is difficult to see how two bodies having to square their decisions with one another could arrive at quicker (or less dirty) conclusions than a single agency with responsibility over the whole field. Criticism of this separation of powers came also from Aubrey Jones, who reminded us that, although the PIB in this country was originally envisaged as having two divisions, this was never observed in practice. 'It is desirable', he writes, 'for the management members of one and the same Board to see and to assume responsibility for the consequences for pay of a decision on prices and profits; and for the trade union members to see and assume responsibility for the consequences on prices of a decision on pay.'[2] But the suspicion remains that the separation of powers was a 'cosmetic' measure, designed under cover of the American precedent, to

1. House of Lords Hansard, 12 March 1973, cols. 31 ff.
2. *The New Inflation*, p.199.

distinguish the Conservative government's proposal from the unitary Prices and Incomes Board established by their predecessors.

Under the new form of incomes policy proposed in later Chapters of this book, the arguments for a single Board have perhaps lost some of their force — except in one important particular, namely that the dyarchy has removed the control of profits from the authority concerned with incomes, and has made this merely incidental to regulation of prices. In so doing it has violated the principle that an equitable incomes policy must take account of its effect on the incomes of individuals, and that, therefore, all personal incomes, whatever their origin, should be dealt with on the same principles.[1]

Policy under the Counter-Inflation Act differed in important respects from the previous government's Prices and Incomes Acts. First, even the change of title may have some significance: the 1973 Act did not profess to do more than contain inflation. In spite of one reference in the Pay Codes to the 'fair' application of their provisions, there was nothing to suggest that the Act had any wider objective in relation to the distribution of incomes. 'Prices and Incomes Acts', on the other hand, might have been expected to have some concern with promoting distributive justice, even if in fact there was little sign of this in their actual terms.

Second, the Pay Board was required to act in conformity with an extremely detailed code, which prescribed the limits of permitted wage or salary increases in precise monetary terms. The Stage 2 Code came into effect at the beginning of April 1973 and was expected to remain (as it did) in force until the autumn, although it carried no terminal date. Wage or salary increases were restricted to a maximum of £1 per head per week + 4% of the

1. This crucial point is discussed further on pp. 48, 49, 86, 87, 96, 97.

average pay bill in the preceding 12 months of the group of workers concerned, with an individual ceiling increase of £250 per annum — a formula which obviously owes so much to the Irish pattern that perhaps it would be more accurate to describe the model as Irish-American rather than pure American. The Code (as also its Stage 3 successor) was therefore a highly legalistic document, defining in great detail just what the pay limit would or would not include by way of incremental scales, advances on promotion, overtime, additional paid holidays and so forth. Indeed it was unofficially suggested that the credit for many of the detailed provisions of the final version was due to Mr. Clive Jenkins of the Scientific, Technical and Managerial Staffs Association, who had boasted that he could find 20 ways of wriggling through loopholes in the first draft. But on any larger issues, or in relation to exceptional cases, the Board was given no room to manoeuvre, as its Reports were from time to time at pains to remind us.

Third, the Pay Board, unlike the PIB, was not authorized to recommend what anybody should be paid.[1] It was restricted to pronouncing on whether proposals submitted to it were, or were not, consistent with the Code, and therefore permissible.

Fourth, inasmuch as profits were treated as margins between costs and selling prices rather than as anybody's personal income, all questions concerning profit limitation were assigned to the Price Commission, not to the Pay Board; and the fees charged 'for professional and other services by firms or by individuals' (e.g. by architects) 'who are self-employed' were similarly referred to the Commission.

Fifth, dividends were not restricted by the Act itself or by the Code, but the Treasury was

---

1. Except on the rare occasions, of which the 1974 Report on the mineworkers was the outstanding example, when its advice was specifically requested by government.

authorized 'to restrict the declaration or payment of ordinary dividends by companies at any time' during the currency of the relevant part of the Act. An Order was accordingly issued to take effect from the beginning of Stage 2 limiting increases in dividends to a maximum of 5% above the level of those paid in the preceding financial year.

Finally, the general principles within which the Board was enjoined to conduct its activities in Stage 2 were much less relevant and explicit than those prescribed for the PIB as will be appreciated if the following rubric is compared with that on pp.40-41. The Pay Board was required

1  to limit the rate of increase in pay in money terms to a level more in line with the growth of national output, so as progressively to reduce the rate of cost and price inflation and improve the prospects of sustained faster growth in real earnings;

2  to apply the limit fairly, irrespective of the form of any increase or the method of determining it;

3  to facilitate an improvement in the relative position of the low paid;

4  to leave to those who normally determine pay decisions on the amount, form and distribution of increases within the limit.

In its application of the first principle, the Board's record is not impressive. In April 1973 the Department of Employment's monthly Index[1] for average weekly earnings of all employees stood at 146.6. By October it had risen to 158.2 which represents an increase of just under 8%. That means that in *the first six months of Stage 2 earnings rose by almost as much as in the six months of no control at all which preceded Stage 1.* The Pay Board itself estimated in its Second Report that the average increase in Stage 2 settlements to the end of August was $7\frac{2}{3}$; but its

1.  January 1970 = 100.

figures exclude the later stages of agreements concluded before Stage 1, so are not fully comprehensive. Even if it is true that during the second half of 1973, until the disastrous industrial disputes at the end of the year, domestic output did show a spurt upwards, the most optimistic estimate would not put this at a level comparable with the increase in earnings. In a review of settlements under Stage 2 to the end of June 1973 by Incomes Data Services,[1] figures for 'latest increases' of between 8% and 10% are common, and increases of between 10% and 20%, especially for women or other low-paid workers, occur not infrequently. For example, 'latest increases' for the lower-paid process workers in steel manufacture were 19.1%; in vehicle body building they ranged from 15.8% for skilled workers to 18.8% for labourers; in the Midlands hosiery finishing trade, from 15.2% for dyers to 16% for the lowest grade; in brush and broom manufacture from 12.5% to 16.3%. Only here and there does an unfortunate group stand out with an increase of 5% or less — such as the top grade of primary school teachers with 3.9%, or the chief nursing officers (among company nurses) with 5.2%. Moreover, later figures issued by the Department of Employment early in 1974 have suggested that the growth of industrial earnings over the whole period from October 1972 to October 1973 may have been as much as 14.2%.[2] On the evidence available, therefore, it does not appear that Stage 2 of the Counter-Inflation policy was any more successful in containing inflation than the Labour government's allegedly 'colossal failure'.

The second of the principles prescribed by the Code might seem, on the face of it, to require the Board to go beyond doing sums about whether or not proposed wages exceeded the permitted limits. The

1. *Incomes Data Services,* Study No. 57, July 1973.
2. *The Times,* 12 February 1974.

danger lies in the word 'fairly' which appears in the formulation of this principle; and those six innocent letters can (and frequently do) paper over a vast chasm of uncertainties. However, the Stage 2 formula was so rigid that the scope for fairness or unfairness in its application could only be minimal, and fundamental issues could therefore easily be dodged. 'Not more than a pound a week for anybody' is a rule so definite that it can only be applied or not applied. What room can there be for degrees of fairness in its application? Moreover, even the definition of the group which in any particular case was to share the 4% addition to the £1 a week was left under paragraph 105 of the Code to the workers concerned; so that in this matter also the Pay Board could not act either fairly or unfairly. But, inevitably, in the long run the fundamental questions of fairness[1] thus evaded by the Stage 2 Code (and also, later, with disastrous results, by its Stage 3 successor) will have to be faced. Nor in this case need the long term be very long. In fact, as will presently appear, the day of reckoning had already arrived before Stage 3 was a month old.

In the interpretation of the third principle, relating to low pay, the primary difficulty is the absence of any definition of 'low'. The Board's chairman, drawing his £16,000 a year, and his colleagues with their £8,000 a year for full-time service and pro-rata payments for part-time attendance, might reasonably have thought that practically every claim that they were asked to consider came from the low paid. But if every claimant was to be relegated to this category, the Board would be unable to give anyone *relative* advantage. A more realistic decision might have been to insist that in every agreement more should be given at the bottom than at the top; and such a tendency was indeed conspicuous in the Stage 2 and Stage 3

1. These are discussed in Chapters IV and V.

Settlements generally. Since, however, the bottom rate in one industry may be above the top in another, this too is not an altogether happy solution. The Board's own Reports (which tend in general to be somewhat uncommunicative) were not forthcoming on this subject. From the first Report we learn only that 'In both the public and the private sectors, settlements have been notified to the Board giving the same cash increases at all levels, or higher percentage increases to the lower paid than would follow from straight application of the £1 + 4% formula'.[1] Three months later[2] it was explained that an increase of £1 +4% gives a larger percentage increase to persons earning a small wage than it does to those at a higher wage; also that the low paid are predominantly women and juveniles, although some adult men are also included; and that 'there is nothing to stop negotiators from concentrating increases on the low paid, if they so wish. '

What effect Stage 2 may have had on the distribution of manpower it is hardly possible to judge. During its currency, complaints about shortages of labour were frequently heard. In the 1973-4 dispute in the coal industry, the loss of men from the pits was indeed a predominant theme in statements by the National Union of Mineworkers, the Coal Board and the Pay Board itself after the mantle of a Relativities Board was thrust upon it.[3] Again, in London and the South of England in general, public services such as transport, teaching, hospital employment and the police force have been in continual trouble through loss of staff or failure to maintain recruitment. No systematic investigation seems, however, to have been undertaken to discover what other industries had benefited from this exodus, or what were the net advantages to the workers concerned of their new, as

1. Pay Board, Report 2 April – 31 May 1973.
2. Pay Board, Second Report 1 June – 31 August 1973.
3. See p.117.

compared with their former, employment. The PIB, as already observed, found the whole subject of the effect of wage-rates upon the distribution of manpower too complex to handle. Obviously there is a danger that adjustment of pay in one industry or occupation in order to discourage employees from migrating elsewhere may lead to bidding and counter-bidding as each employment tries to rival the attractions of the other. Nor is it enough to analyse the situation at one end only. If any necessary adjustments of pay are to be quantified, as in the end they must be, investigations have to be made into what volume of employment is desirable in both the losing and the receiving industries, as well as into the level of earnings in each case. The questions 'Where have all the workers gone, and why?' imperatively demand answers; but they can only be answered by highly sophisticated calculations, and even when these have been made, large gaps (e.g. in regard to the scale of the relativities necessary to effect any desired redistribution) will remain.

In this connection Derek Robinson, a Deputy Chairman of the Pay Board, has suggested[1] that 'A more rational, less inflationary, way of tackling manpower and wages problems must consider labour allocation'; and that there may have to be more 'geographical or industrial or occupational mobility which would be induced by non-wage factors'; but, regrettably, he added no concrete proposals as to how this might be achieved.

In October 1973 the imminent demise of Stage 2 was heralded by the publication of a 'Consultative Document' containing a first draft of the Stage 3 Code. In the introduction to this draft the government proudly boasted that, although the 'surge in world prices' was without precedent in the previous

1. Robinson, Derek. *Incomes Policy and Capital Sharing in Europe* (Croom Helm, 1973), p.72.

73

twenty years, they had succeeded in Stages 1 and 2 'in restraining the domestic causes of inflation'. If this meant that inflation would have been even greater if there had been no controls on pay at all, it may well have been true of both Stage 1 and Stage 2; but if it implied that the first principle of the Pay Code — that is, 'the limitation of the rate of increase in pay in money terms to a level more in line with the growth of national output' — if that was the implication, the claim was highly questionable in relation to Stage 2. As the figures on p.69 show, the rate of increase in earnings was at least as high in Stage 2 as it had been in the six months when no statutory controls were in force at all.

About a month later the ill-fated Stage 3 Code became operative, having undergone some modifications, mostly in the direction of reduced stringency, since the appearance of the first draft in the Consultative Document. At two points amendments had been made to the 'general principles' of pay as written into Stage 2. First, the words 'while providing for the remedying of anomalies' were added to the instruction to the Board to apply the pay limit 'fairly'; and, second, an additional clause was inserted, directing the Board to 'encourage the better use of productive resources'.

Of these amendments, the first was consequential upon the Report on Anomalies which the Board had produced in September 1973 at governmental request. The definition of anomalies in this context was, however, very tightly drawn, being confined to cases arising from the 'impact of the previous standstill', in cases where pay had been, 'determined by links with the settlements of other groups or by formal procedures for comparing their pay with that of others'.[1] Inevitably therefore the

1. Terms of Reference of the Pay Board's Report on Anomalies, Cmnd 5429 of 1973.

findings of the Anomalies Report were essentially
conservative. The freeze had disturbed traditional
relativities inasmuch as some settlements had been
agreed before the ice hardened, while others that
were still in process of negotiation were caught with
their pay frozen where it stood. The Stage 3 Code
accordingly included clauses permitting the implementation of these frozen agreements, provided that
they did not exceed the Stage 3 pay limit; and in
addition it opened the door to the rectification of
anomalies resulting from cases in which the traditional links between the pay of certain groups of
workers had been broken by the freeze. This door,
however, was very carefully guarded by definitions of
what in this context would qualify as a genuine link.

The second addendum to the governing principles
of the Code, which required the Board to encourage
'the better use of productive resources' was presumably a hint to pay attention to questions of the
distribution of manpower. Since, however, the Board
was in its own words empowered only[1] 'to ascertain
the facts and to act as interpreters of the statutory
rules', it is difficult to see what it could have done to
comply with this injunction.

Apart from these innovations the Stage 3 Code was
in general a somewhat relaxed version of Stage 2 and,
like its predecessor, it carried no terminal date. A new
formula, allowing increases of £2.25 per head per
week or (not 'and' as previously) 7% for the group,
subject to a £350 ceiling for individual increases,
replaced the previous pay limit. In addition the rules
for extra payments for what have come to be known
as 'unsocial hours' (i.e. night, rest day and weekend
working) were re-written so as to enable more
workers to take advantage of them; an extra 1% of
the average pay per head of a group was permitted as
a 'flexibility margin' to cover re-structuring of pay

1. Pay Board, Third Report, 1 September – 30 November 1973.

systems or the cost of improvements in holiday or sick pay; conditions were prescribed for allowing payments above the limit under new efficiency schemes; and the door was opened to payment of London allowances in accordance with a formula adopted by the PIB six years earlier. But probably the most important change of all was the concession made to 'threshold arrangements', which provided that when the Department of Employment's Retail Price Index rose by 7% above the figure for October 1973 an additional pay increase of up to 40p per week would be permissible, and thereafter further such increases would be allowable for every subsequent 1% rise of the index in excess of 7%. These arrangements, it must be understood, were not to be automatically applicable to everybody, but only became operative in those cases in which they had been expressly included in collective agreements.

The inclusion of this last provision in an allegedly counter-inflationary programme seems quite extraordinary. (Incidentally it was in remarkable contrast to the protection against inflation afforded to retirement pensioners, whose pensions were at the time subject only to annual review — later shortened to six months — whereas the price index is published every month, and wages under threshold agreements during Stage 3 could therefore be adjusted at similar intervals.) In any serious attempt to counter inflation, it must surely be crazy to introduce into wage regulation a factor which would be guaranteed to reactivate the vicious circle of wages chasing prices-chasing wages. 'Threshold arrangements' moreover were not even proposed as a sop to the unions, who in fact expressed relentless opposition to them, presumably on the ground that they would violate the hitherto unchallengeable law that money wages ought in all circumstances to be increased *faster* than the cost of living, so that real standards may be continuously raised. Yet as far back as the nineteen-twenties, cost-of-living arguments had been the regular stock-in-trade of almost every wage claim; and a number of agreements had provided for automatic increases linked to retail prices. Gradually, however, these had died out, and the PIB at an early stage in its history frowned so severely on claims based on this criterion that thereafter 'there were very few cases in which rises in the cost of living were advanced as justification for a wage increase'.[1] One can only suppose that their reappearance in the Stage 3 Code justified the suspicions of the unions, inasmuch as, by providing for automatic cost-of-living increases, the government hoped to be able to resist claims for still further advances over and above those approved on this ground.

Stage 3, however, immediately ran into such appallingly heavy weather as a result of the 1973-4 miners' and railwaymen's disputes that no general assessment of its potentialities is possible. It was indeed ironic that no sooner had the injunction 'to encourage the better use of productive resources' been added to the general principles of pay, than industry was restricted to a three-day week. Within weeks the new Code had become an object of political, rather than economic, significance, and, though it was only one of an annual flow of hundreds of similar Orders and, as such, subject to revocation by Parliament at any time, nevertheless in the eyes of its authors (and many others) it was treated with a veneration more appropriate to a commandment graven upon stone than to an ephemeral Statutory Instrument. Its eventual fate at the time of writing (May 1974) is not yet known, but since legislation to abolish the Pay Board is already in course of preparation, Stage 3 must be regarded as under

1. Fels, Allan. *The British Prices and Incomes Board* (Cambridge University Press, 1972) p.105.

sentence of death, and will presumably have passed away before these words appear in print. So long, however, as it survives, one prediction can be confidently made: if Stage 2 failed to 'limit the rate of increase of pay to a level more in line with the growth of national output', Stage 3 was inexorably doomed to even more conspicuous failure — and on two counts, both because it conceded larger increases of pay and because any growth of national output shrank to vanishing point.

Whatever the future may hold, it is clear that both the Labour and the Conservative experiments had some failings in common. Both were restricted by their limited vision which compelled them to stagger from emergency to emergency, or from 'stage' to 'stage'. Both ignored the ethical problems involved in the distribution of income between individuals. Both treated all shareholders alike whatever their addresses or bank balances, and both allowed large speculative profits to escape their control altogether.

At the same time there were also significant differences between the two policies. The PIB had been authorized to make definite recommendations about the legitimacy of proposed price or wage increases. In so doing, it was given a definite norm to work to, and a list of conditions for exceptional treatment which would in certain circumstances justify some excess over the norm; and its members were called upon to judge in what cases those conditions were satisfied and how great that excess should be. The reasons for its conclusions on particular cases were argued at length in reports which were subsequently published; and in addition to these reports it produced also a number of others of great value dealing with matters of principle relevant to wage determination. On the other hand the PIB was, as already mentioned, restricted (not to say frustrated, as some of its ex-members have since revealed) by having no control over its own agenda and no power to enforce its recommendations.

The Pay Board found itself in the exactly opposite situation. It had absolute power or no power at all, according to how one looked at it. The power was absolute inasmuch as any agreement which the Board declared to be in breach of the current Code became illegal and unenforceable — although there might be subsequent discussion between the parties and the Board as to how their proposals could be modified so as to comply with the Code's requirements. On the other hand, the Board had no discretionary power whatever, (until its metamorphosis during the 1974 miners' strike)[1] because it was imprisoned in a mass of extremely detailed regulations not of its own making. Whereas the PIB had wide powers to treat as exceptional cases the categories listed under its terms of reference, the Stage 2 and Stage 3 Codes allowed its successor no comparable freedom. The payments listed as 'not counting against the pay limit' had to do with shift working, promotions, overtime or such like, and served only, so to speak, as definitions of the limits of the limit. As such they applied equally to everybody, whether he was well or badly paid, without regard to the national importance of his work. Consequently the most that the Board could do for exceptional cases was to see whether the rules could be stretched by any lawyers' tricks.

This in turn had the result that the 'general principles of pay' which headed the Pay Code were really quite irrelevant. In its Second Report the Board itself made the point that it had 'no power to depart from the provisions of the Code on grounds of fairness' — a doctrine which was further underlined in Lord Justice Lawton's judgment in January 1974 in a case in which two employees of two firms in the china clay industry claimed for arrears of pay under a

1. See p.117.

productivity agreement which had been agreed with their respective employers (who deemed it to be non-inflationary) but was turned down by the Board. Summarizing the position his Lordship said that the Board had decided that 'they had to apply the code strictly and rigidly, and did not purport to exercise any discretion because of the alleged counter-inflationary aspects' of the proposed agreements. . . . 'The employers invited the board to adapt and modify the code to enable the principles to be applied to the pay and salaries procedures in the industry'. . . . In his Lordship's view the employers' argument was misconceived. 'Their fundamental error lay in thinking that the board could exercise any dispensing power.'[1]

The absurdities, not to say the dangers, of these legalistic swaddling clothes were clearly illustrated by two incidents. The first occurred during the miners' dispute in 1973-4. There came a point when it appeared to be widely held that the miners ought to have better wages than those of the Coal Board's current offer, even though this would mean breaching the current pay limit. But why? To that question sympathetic members of the public would answer: because miners' work is hard, dirty and dangerous and they are less well paid than many other workers whose conditions are much pleasanter; or because miners have dropped several places in recent years in the table of earnings: or because, with the shortage of oil, coal has become immensely important to our economy, and miners are leaving the industry in search of better wages just when they are most urgently needed in the pits: or because the pay of some at least of the mineworkers cannot be said to give them a reasonable standard of living. These were the *real* reasons why many people were persuaded of the justice of the miners' claim. Members of the

1. *The Times*, 19 January 1974.

public interviewed on radio or television were repeatedly heard to say that they 'wouldn't want to do that sort of work, even for £100 a week'. Moreover the reasons given were all grounds on which the PIB could, if it had found them convincing, have recommended that the claim should be allowed. But the Stage 3 Code had never heard of any of them. None of these arguments could be urged upon the Pay Board because the Board would be *ultra vires* in even considering them. So what happened? Without mentioning the real reasons for supporting the claim, desperate efforts were made to find possible reinterpretations of the Code's formulae in order to see if these could be stretched to cover an increase which would still be technically within the immovable and immutable pay limit. For example: if the limit restricted the wage payable for time spent in normal working, could not the miner be deemed to be working when he was bathing?

The plain fact was that either the miners deserved more money (for the real reasons) or they did not. If they did, then they should be entitled to it, without the silliness of having to resort to ingenious verbal gymnastics in order to extract irrelevant justifications from an irrelevant document. In the end, as recounted in Chapter V of this book, the Pay Board was instantaneously released from its bondage by being transmuted, for the purpose of settling this particular dispute, into a Relativities Board with a virtually limitless discretion to recommend whatever solution it might think appropriate, though without any power to enforce this.

The second incident was of rather a different character. It relates to the case of Sir John Stratton,[1] chairman of one of Europe's largest meat wholesaling concerns. The Stage 2 Code contained an innocent-looking clause which allowed profit-sharing schemes

1. Incomes Data Services, Report 171, October 1973.

as they stood before 6 November 1972 not to count against the pay limit. No doubt the authors of the Code envisaged the kind of schemes under which employees receive a modest bonus at Christmas or perhaps quarterly. But Sir John, who was paid a basic salary plus commission on his firm's results, became entitled to a rise of £16,416, bringing his total remuneration to £53,433 for the year. True, it was his first rise for 14 years, but even so it is hardly surprising that it created considerable resentment and cynicism amongst workers whose claims for a few extra pounds a week were being rejected; and it was particularly unfortunate that such an incident should occur to the benefit of someone engaged in meat trading at a time when the price of beef was going through the roof. But the rules were the rules and the Board could do nothing about them (though Sir John did announce that he would give the money to charity).

As a result of this incident a clause was at the last minute added to the Stage 3 Draft Code, providing that no person was to receive in any year more than £350 (the normal maximum individual increase allowed under the Code) above what 'would be due if profits or turnover were at the average level of the best two of the preceding 5 years' (that is, the 'reference level'). This, however, left the door fairly wide open in cases where 'the best two' had been very good years, and subsequently two further, equally startling, cases came to light. In February 1974 Mr. John Boardman, Chairman of a firm of building contractors, is reported[1] to have received an increase of £15,500 or 172% of his annual salary. This he 'believed to be within the limits of the pay code'; but he and his fellow directors are said to have waived further increases of more than £52,000. In the same

1. *The Times*, 1 February 1974.
2. 15 February 1974.

month, according to a radio report,[2] Sir John Rank also received an increase of £15,000 bringing his salary up to £65,000 p.a; but again this was his first increase for eight years; and 'he would have waived it, but for the effect on his pension rights'.

This comparison of the PIB's position and that of the Pay Board should drive home the lesson that any long-term policy must avoid excessive rigidity on the one hand, and undue laxity on the other: also (and this is just the other side of the same problem) that it is important to draw the line in the right place as between matters of policy which must be decided by government, and consequential decisions which should be left to those responsible for reviewing or drafting actual settlements. As Professor Clegg has observed, the rules under which the PIB operated offered plenty of loopholes; but after experience of the tightly drawn Codes of Stages 2 and 3, we may perhaps conclude that a garment disfigured by holes is to be preferred to a strait-jacket — provided only that the holes are not too large, or in unsuitable places.

1. *How to run an Incomes Policy* p.14.

# IV

# Outline Proposal for an
# Incomes Gains Tax

THE INQUEST is now completed, with a verdict of death from short-sightedness in relation both to the long-term future and to the equitable treatment of individuals in the present. But in spite of all their inadequacies and mistakes, the Labour and Conservative experiments had between them one significant achievement to record. They succeeded in familiarising the public with the idea of an incomes policy; and as not infrequently happens, familiarity in due course showed signs of breeding acceptance. In the survey conducted in January 1974 by Opinion Research Centre for *New Society*,[1] 47% of the respondents expressed 'an unconditional willingness to accept' a statutory limitation corresponding to the Stage 3 pay limit; and this figure would have risen to 79% if the government could make sure that prices were kept steady – though considerable doubts were expressed about the feasibility of this condition being satisfied. On the general merits of an incomes policy, 60% felt that it was likely to make Britain 'a fairer and better place' to live in, as against only 44% who had expressed this view in a similar survey in 1967. To the question whether they thought that they would themselves be better off under an incomes policy 37%, as against 20% in 1967, gave affirmative answers. Finally, although the survey did not specifically differentiate the opinions of trade unionists, the 'social contract' between the TUC and the Labour government itself implied acceptance at least of the principle of an incomes

1. referred to on p.92 below.

policy, even if only of a voluntary character.

The next step therefore is to devise a long-term policy which will be at once equitable and economically viable. First, as to equity: references to 'fairness' or social justice are freely scattered through the policy documents and legislative instruments relating to the two British experiments in statutory control of incomes, and they are even more liberally employed in the speeches of politicians, businessmen, trade unionists and the like. 'Fair' seems indeed to have been Edward Heath's favourite word (especially as applied to his own government's policies) in the February 1974 Election campaign.[1] But definitions of exactly what constitutes justice or fairness are less conspicuous. (After all Socrates was put to death for making a fuss about this very question.) If only everybody's income arrived regularly by post without any regard to what he might or might not have done to earn it, there would be no problem. In that case justice would not even need both halves of the formula: 'from each according to his ability, to each according to his need'. The second half alone would be sufficient, and it would be difficult to dispute that justice would then call for an equal distribution, modified only by the special needs of those who suffered from handicaps involving unavoidable extra expense. But in the real world people get their incomes in a variety of ways and most people get them from different sources at different times of life. In this country at any given moment about 70% of personal income comes from working for an employer, about 9% from self-employment, about 10% from rent, interest and dividends, and about 11% from social security payments; nor do these figures vary much from year to year, the main change over the past twenty years being a slow decline in incomes

1. See Blumler, Jay G. The Media and the Election, *New Society*, 7 March 1974.

from self-employment, balanced by an increase in those derived from social security.Fairness therefore involves highly contentious issues concerning the relationship between income received and the way in which a title to it is established, whether by work or otherwise.

As we have seen, our two experiments in statutory incomes policy were at one in treating each of the above categories of income separately. Increases in wages and salaries were expected in general to conform to a 'norm' under Labour's policy, but this could be overridden on the recommendation of the PIB, acting within prescribed rules. Under the Conservatives' Counter-Inflation Acts wage and salary increases were subject to the Pay Board's certification that they fell within the limits of the Stage 2 or Stage 3 formula as the case might be. Both schemes restricted dividend distributions by direct governmental control based on a maximum percentage increase over the level of the preceding year. Neither imposed restrictions on business profits or the incomes of self-employed persons as such, these being treated as incidental to the prices or fees charged for goods and services; but, whereas under the earlier scheme these categories were subject to review by the PIB, which was itself also responsible for investigations into wages, under the Counter-Inflation Acts the incomes of self-employed persons in business or the professions were assigned to the Price Commission, and not to the Pay Board.

These last provisions reflect, I suggest, a fundamental flaw in both policies, because they made it impossible to estimate the comparative effect of the restrictions upon individuals in every single category and at every level of income. Justice, by whatever criterion it may be assessed, always requires that like be compared with like, or that comparisons between groups or individuals should relate only to characteristics that they have in common. A railway locomotive may be compared with a bicycle in respect of weight, or the speed at which each can travel, or the quantity of steel required for their respective manufacture. But an undifferentiated comparison of a locomotive with a bicycle is meaningless. Equally meaningless, from the point of view of social justice, is any comparison between the recipients of dividends (whether rich or poor) as a class with the whole class of (rich or poor) wage and salary earners. By definition a comprehensive incomes policy must modify the existing distribution of income. But the justice of any change in the distribution of income can only be assessed if it is related to the way in which income is already distributed, not between categories, but between persons, since the persons comprised in each category stand at widely separated points in respect of the incomes that they already enjoy. There are rich shareholders and poor shareholders, employees drawing thousands a year and others with less than £20 a week. If therefore a policy is to satisfy any concept of social justice it must take account of the actual income of actual persons, and relate its proposals to its effect both upon the pattern of distribution as a whole, and upon the special claims of particular groups to differential treatment, as well as upon the efficient functioning of the economy.

To achieve this will demand an entirely new approach to the design of a policy that is to be more than a temporary emergency measure intended essentially as a bulwark against inflation, though decorated with occasional concessions to 'social justice'. Since the data about individual incomes upon which such a policy must be based are available in one place, and only one place — that is, in the offices of the Inland Revenue — it follows that the policy must be integrated into, and operated through, the tax system. Only the tax gatherer knows (or should know) what goes into the pocket or bank account of each and every one of us. Was it therefore prophetic, if unconscious, insight which led both the Conservative and the Labour governments, in their references to the need to control profits and dividends as well as incomes from employment, to use the word 'fiscal' in that constantly repeated formula about employing 'fiscal or other appropriate means' to prevent any excessive growth in aggregate profits? — even though in practice under both governments 'fiscal' gave way to 'other' means, the appropriateness of which turned out to be decidedly questionable.

*My own proposal is therefore that we should introduce a long-term incomes policy by means of a comprehensive Incomes Gains Tax (hereafter referred to as IGT) to match the Capital Gains Tax that we already have.* While the operation of such a tax is discussed in more detail in the Chapters that follow, its two basic principles would be first, that in any year the aggregate allowable increase in personal incomes would be related to the increase in available domestic output in the preceding 12 months. Although it would no doubt be tempting to base the norm on the expected rise in productivity in the coming year rather than on the realised achievement of the past, experience has shown that such estimates are so much at the mercy of unforeseen events and of unconquerable optimism, that the temptation ought to be firmly resisted, and the rise in aggregate money incomes kept in step with the already recorded growth of productivity. Second, individual taxpayers would be permitted, free of IGT, a maximum percentage increase in their existing incomes after payment of income tax and other statutory deductions. Any excess over this permitted increase would be subject to 100% tax. If this sounds excessively severe, it should be remembered, first, that the absolute limits set by the Stage 2 and Stage 3 Codes on increases in wage-earners' incomes were equivalent to 100% tax on any excess over these limits; and, second, that restriction of company dividends to 5% above the level of the preceding year was equivalent, from the shareholder's point of view, to the imposition of 100% tax on any excess over 5%. The 100% tax is simply an alternative (and as I hope to show a preferable) method of achieving exactly the same result as a prescribed statutory limit on any increase of incomes.

In the first instance the individual taxpayer's entitlement to an IGT-free increase of income would be graduated ('primary grading') according to the magnitude of his existing net income after payment of income tax and other statutory deductions. While IGT would be collected along with income tax, that is to say, on a weekly basis in the case of persons paid by the week, it would be assessed on the average earnings of the preceding year, so as to avoid the complications and possible inequities that might arise in the case of workers whose earnings fluctuated widely – as often happens – from week to week. Net income after payment of income tax would be the appropriate basis of assessment, inasmuch as one of the objects of the whole exercise would be to control any inflationary expansion of personal spending power. For the sake of simplicity also IGT exemptions should be calculated as percentages on existing net income, not on a flat rate basis such as was included in the pay limit under the Stage 2 and Stage 3 Codes. In a long-term policy a flat rate exemption would be inappropriate, since with the changing value of money it would quickly become out of date, and it would also complicate the problem of calculating what scale of exemption could be afforded without aggravating inflation. Finally it must be emphasized that, while IGT would prevent any increase in net personal income above a prescribed figure, that would in no way guarantee that such increases would be automatically achieved. Within the IGT limit, economic pressures and wage bargaining would continue to operate.

When it comes to settling the shape of the primary grading of IGT, the crucial question of what is meant by 'social justice' or 'fairness' can no longer be evaded. In what direction, we must therefore ask, do we wish to modify the present pattern of incomes? Ought there to be a level below which nobody ought to fall and/or a ceiling above which nobody should rise? Are we or are we not content with the assumption that what would be regarded as chicken-feed for the professional classes is affluence for the manual worker? Obviously these are, and must be, matters of opinion: no demonstrably correct answers are possible; and opinions on the subject will necessarily reflect social and ethical valuations. The tax could be graded so as to make the spread of incomes wider than it is at present by allowing larger increases in the higher ranges than lower down; or conversely it could be used as an instrument for reducing existing inequalities. It follows that the grading of IGT is a subject for political controversy and should properly be decided, as should all social decisions involving ethical issues, at a political level. Since references to 'social justice' and 'fairness' do not mean the same to everybody, they must, if they are to be reflected in fiscal policy, be open to public discussion, be explicitly formulated by the government of the day and be subject to Parliamentary scrutiny. They are indeed the stuff of which the great debates of politics are made, and are the concern, not of experts but of Everyman, and to Everyman the politicians must be answerable for them.

To provide material for this debate a glance at an outline of the existing distribution of net income

90

after payment of income tax may be useful.[1]
According to the Inland Revenue, there were in
1970-71 (latest available figures[2]) 21,368,000
recipients of personal incomes. (Actually the total
number of personal incomes is substantially larger,
because the Revenue authorities, being theologically
orthodox, regard man and wife as one flesh, or at
least as statistically sharing one income whether
acquired by either or both of them). Between
them, these 21 million income-receivers shared a
net total, after payment of income tax, of £26,846.9
million. Of this total 12,339,000 persons (or
married couples) with up to £1,000 a year took
£10,115.0 million and 9,029,000 persons (or married
couples) with more than £1,000 a year took
£16,731.9 million. If we suppose that the available
aggregate of personal incomes in the following year
rose by 5%, that would give an additional £1,342.34
million to be distributed; and if it was further decided
that the first claim on that should be a 10% rise for
everybody with up to £1,000 a year that would take
£1,011.5 million, leaving only £330.84 million to be
shared by those above the £1,000 a year level, which
would only allow them a rise of less than 2%. We
have, therefore, to face the fact, illustrated by this
hypothetical example, that the proportion of people
in the lower ranges of income is so large that any
serious attempt to improve their position must mean
that everybody else must be prepared to get little or
nothing extra.

Contemporary reactions to this picture vary. On
the 20 January 1974 Sir Keith Joseph expressed on
television his personal opinion that, while the unequal
distribution of wealth was still a matter for concern,

1. This is, of course, very much less unequal than the distribution of
   pre-tax income.
2. Later figures would show substantially larger absolute amounts of
   income, but it is unlikely that the overall distribution would be
   appreciably different.

the trend towards equalisation of income had gone far enough. Other prominent personalities have, however, been more critical. A week later Lord Robens, also on television, made an incidental comment in a discussion on trade unions to the effect that none of us, in his judgment, believes that the national cake is fairly shared. On the radio on 21 January 1974 Mr. Campbell Adamson of the CBI urged, in connection with the miners' dispute, that we should sit down and seriously consider a fairer system of distribution of wealth and income; and he made it clear that he had in mind that this must include a review of the whole system as it affects employers as well as their employees. On 1 November 1973, Mr. Bernard Levin in *The Times* wrote that 'We have got to start thinking now, with the utmost possible urgency, of ways to ensure that those who do the dirty work get·a financial reward that bears some relation to its nature and the need for it', – and he also ascribed some of the angry feelings then prevalent to 'the realisation that we must move, with all deliberate speed, towards something much more like equality, if our society is not to disintegrate under the pressure of those at the bottom of the ladder'. Finally, on the 19th of the same month Sir Fred Catherwood expressed similar opinions, though somewhat less dramatically, on the radio.

That such diverse voices should be singing in unison is surely remarkable. It would seem also that they have a supporting chorus behind them. The survey (already quoted) of public attitudes on pay and inflation undertaken by Opinion Research Centre found that 74% of the sample questioned felt that there was 'too great a difference in this country between the pay of people in top jobs and the pay of people in bottom jobs'.[1] Nor should it be overlooked,

1. Fosh, Patricia and Jackson, Dudley. Pay Policy and Inflation: *What Britain Thinks,* New Society, 7 February 1974.

92

first, that both the Conservative and the Labour Party include the mitigation, if not the abolition, of poverty amongst their objectives, although the Labour Party is troubled, as the Tories apparently are not, by the co-existence of rags and riches; second, that the statutory policies of both governments specifically enjoined that special treatment should be given to the low-paid; and, third, that many of the Stage 2 and Stage 3 settlements bear witness that this injunction did not fall everywhere on deaf ears. Add all this together, and the stream of criticism directed against the present distribution of income begins to look pretty formidable.

In what follows, as a life-long adherent of an equalitarian philosophy, I shall assume that the primary grading of IGT will be such as to reduce inequality by allowing larger IGT-free exemptions, and therefore larger increases in net income, in the lower than in the upper ranges of incomes. My particular version of an IGT proposal will therefore be likely to commend itself more to the Left than to the Right. But I must again remind those who find this unpalatable, that the principle of an IGT has nothing to do with the particular grading proposed. Those who dislike my philosophy can perfectly well design an alternative grading which (though in my view inequitable) would produce an exactly opposite influence upon the distribution of income, without in any way impairing the tax's anti-inflationary effect. But from this point on I shall assume an equalitarian standpoint.

In the contemporary climate this philosophy tends to have more of a social than an economic flavour, and owes perhaps more to day-by-day observation of the life-styles of different sections of the community, than to statistics such as those quoted on p.91. It is not only that the lavish parties and luxurious homes and cars of the very rich are constantly flaunted

93

before our eyes on television and in the Press: less extreme contrasts are also significant, and to those who share my own philosophy these are little, if at all, less distasteful. The comfortable residences of suburbia are an insult to the slum dweller, as are the absurdly sumptuous window displays of the high-class shopping districts to the great majority who may gaze but cannot buy. Yet one does not have to be a millionaire to live in such a residence or to patronise those shops from time to time: the income of a higher civil servant or a professor will suffice. But to the three million of our fellow citizens who must subsist on supplementary benefit, such life-styles are as inaccessible as the moon.

It is because gross inequalities of wealth and income shape the whole social pattern that they are so objectionable — and so divisive. More than any other factor these inequalities perpetuate the class structure of our society, which is not, as some would have it, undermined by mobility between classes. The contrasts remain, even if some individuals end up in a different stratum from that in which they started. Subtle differences in social conventions, in attitudes, and in ethical standards still inhibit social intercourse and mutual understanding across class barriers. Indeed the industrial unrest of to-day may well be due more to class segregation and its consequential differences in life-styles than to any sinister plots against democratic government; and this may be the key to the militancy of those trade unionists who now challenge, as never before, our deep-seated (if generally tacit) assumptions as to the appropriate relation of manual to professional pay. When miners even talk of reaching £4,000 a year, that must be the end of middle class references to the 'high wages' of factory workers at £50 a week.

To return to IGT; if this is to achieve its twin objectives of both modifying inequality of income and containing inflation, two factors will be crucial. First the total sum available for increasing incomes, if we are not to revert to the practice of trying to live off paper money, is unlikely to be substantial in the foreseeable future. Even discounting the dismal atmosphere of early 1974 in which these words are written, and the possibility that the increase in domestic production for that year will at best be negligible, a sustained growth rate of 5% p.a. is as much as, probably more than, can normally be expected. Indeed, if any significant — and visible — reduction of inequality is to be achieved, it will undoubtedly be necessary, owing to the preponderance of small incomes already illustrated, to allow no further increase at all in incomes at a point well below the highest level at present attainable. In the examples that follow on pp.149-51 I have suggested that, with the value of money and direct taxes somewhere near their early 1974 level, this ceiling might be fixed at £5,000 p.a. after payment of income tax. But even this was based on optimistic assumptions which seem unlikely to be realised to-morrow; indeed only a dramatic improvement in the country's prosperity would make it possible for an IGT limit for nil exemption to be set even as high as a net income of £5,000 p.a. One can only say that the detailed graduation of IGT scales must be a matter for political judgment from time to time in the light of the current growth of domestic output and the prevailing conceptions of social justice, and that the more radical the approach, the lower the ceiling would be set and the more generous could be the exemptions at the bottom of the scale.

One inevitable result of fixing any figure beyond which no increase would be permissible would be that above this level IGT would not directly reduce inequality of income. Indirectly, it should have an appreciable equalising effect, inasmuch as it would make the ladder to the highest levels harder to climb: there would be no more cases of tycoons with (pre-tax) incomes of, say, £40,000 a year getting rises to £50,000 or more. But at these levels income tax would in any case seem a more appropriate instrument than IGT for reducing inequalities. Also, as already suggested, the occasional peaks of very high incomes are perhaps less socially deplorable than the much more general contrasts between the poor and the fairly well-to-do, if only because it is these contrasts which raise the really insurmountable barriers. Industrial magnates with £70,000 a year (gross) will dine and wine, and their children will intermarry, with the £5,000 − £10,000 class: but persons at the level of supplementary benefit or family income supplement do not normally mix and marry with those whose incomes reach even the £5,000 mark.

A tax which merely modified the overall distribution of income so as to reduce inequality would, however, be unlikely fully to satisfy either current conceptions of social justice or the demands of economic necessity. There are still to be considered (in the Chapters that follow) the special cases of workers claiming that their work is undervalued and that they should be entitled to larger IGT exemptions than others in the same income-bracket, together with sundry problems relating to the scope and structure of IGT. But to conclude this outline it may be worth recording here three substantial advantages inherent in IGT (and indeed in any incomes policy operated through the tax system) which are independent of its actual graduation.

First, coverage would be completely comprehensive. Speculators, people running their own businesses, landlords living on rents, company directors, shareholders, as well as every grade of wage or salary-earners would come within its purview; and in this it would be unique. Quite apart from the anomalous treatment of dividends and profits under both the Labour and the Conservative governments' legislation, the 1973 Counter-Inflation Act did not even take cognizance of all wage incomes. Under this Act the Pay Board was empowered to restrict 'any kind of remuneration' and for this purpose the Secretary of State for Employment was authorized to issue Orders requiring notification of new wage settlements. Since, however, it would obviously be impossible for the Board to examine every single agreement that might be made throughout the length and breadth of the land, in the first instance only settlements involving 1,000 or more persons had to be notified and approved before being implemented. Those involving between 100 and 1,000 employees had to be reported within 7 days of implementation, but firms with between 10 and 100 employees were only required to keep records, whilst those employing less than 10 persons were merely exhorted in general terms to observe the Pay Code, without any obligation either to make reports or to keep records. Information as to the number of firms employing less than 100 employees not being available, it is not possible accurately to estimate the quantitative effect of these limitations, but it may well be considerable. In June 1972 just over 200,000 'census units' (which are more numerous and on the average smaller than firms) with between 11 and 99 employees were registered in Gt. Britain, and these employed a total of just over 6 million workers[1] exclusive of those engaged in agriculture and private domestic service. Since the Inland Revenue is as much interested in workers employed in small enterprises as in those working in large undertakings, IGT would close this gap.

Second, because IGT would be a personal tax, it

1. House of Lords Hansard, 24 October 1973, col. 735.

would treat all individuals on the same basis, and its equity or inequity as between one taxpayer and another could therefore be assessed. As already pointed out, the method in which the Counter-Inflation Codes handle business profits and dividends makes this impossible in relation to recipients of these categories of income.

Third, existing administrative machinery could be utilised to make the policy effective. Tax evasion may occur, but at least machinery for dealing with it exists and is regularly used. Anyone who contrived to evade his IGT liability would therefore be dealt with in the same way as any income tax dodger, and we should thus escape the absurdities of both the Labour and the Conservative legislation in respect of enforcement. Not only did the Labour government fail to initiate a single prosecution for offences under the 1966-8 Acts: subsequently the Conservatives faithfully followed suit. Although under the Counter-Inflation Acts the financial penalties were modestly upgraded, and incitements as well as actual contraventions included in the list of offences, yet at least down to the end of 1973 under these Acts also not a single person or organisation had been prosecuted. One can only conclude that both governments were content to leave the enforcement of their policies to paper tigers. But not so the Inland Revenue authorities. Though often very patient, they at least can be relied upon to bring persistent defaulters to book in the end.

# V

# Incomes Gains Tax:
# Treatment of Special Cases

A S SO FAR outlined IGT might control domestic inflation and diminish inequality: but it would not touch the major problem which has hitherto been the chief concern of incomes policies — namely the relationship of pay to the nature of the work by which it is earned. Graduation of IGT merely by the size of the taxpayer's income would undoubtedly provoke outcries from workers contending that they are already wrongly placed on the ladder, and should be entitled to larger increases than others on the same rung. Relativities would rear their awkward heads and demand to be incorporated into the structure of IGT.

That demand must be met. For that purpose it will be necessary, first, to take a brief look at a few illustrations of the present pattern of wages and salaries; second, to consider how this has come to be what it is; and third to identify areas in which it could and should be modified; and finally to design the machinery by which any necessary modification can be incorporated in the structure of IGT. Incidentally, on all these issues except the last, the argument of this chapter as to the identification of 'special cases' has a relevance that extends beyond the particular question of IGT grading and is equally applicable to any form of control of wages and salaries. Since the problems to be discussed are common to all statutory incomes policies, this search for solutions may perhaps also be of common interest.

Twenty years ago I included in *The Social Foundations of Wage Policy* a chapter on 'Curiosities of British Wage Structure'. To-day if that structure has not become, in the language of *Alice in Wonderland* 'curiouser and curiouser', it certainly exhibits features which are not easy either to comprehend or to justify. So far as official sources are concerned the best evidence is to be found in the Department of Employment's New Earnings Survey[1] which regularly records the average weekly earnings of manual working men in each of 27 main industrial classes. In April 1973 this gave the average for all industries as £38.1. Top of the list at that date were men employed in vehicle building and repairing at an average of £44.2 per week, closely followed by the paper, printing and publishing industries at £44.1. These groups were (and are) the aristocrats of the manual working world; but not far below them came workers in coal and petroleum products at £42.2; in shipbuilding at £42.0; in bricks, pottery and glass manufacture at £40.3; in transport and communications at £40.2 — with coal miners just behind at £39.7. At the other end of the scale were workers in distributive services at £32.2; in public administration at £31.1; in miscellaneous service trades at £30.3; and in agriculture at £29.5.

Non-manual workers, as would be expected, ranked decidedly higher. Men employed in banking, insurance and similar services took first place at £55 p.w., followed by those engaged in chemical and allied industries at £53.1, in the paper, printing and publishing group at £51.4, and in electrical engineering at £50.2. The vehicle builders and repairers were down to fifth place at £49.7; the professional and scientific group stood at £49.5 and transport and communications at £48.9. At the lower end of the non-manual scales were those employed in the iron and steel industry at £45.4, workers in miscellaneous services at £43; and bottom of the list employees in the distributive trades at £41.1. The spread from top

1. *Department of Employment Gazette*, November 1973.

to bottom, it will be observed, is noticeably less for non-manual than for manual workers; and neither the ranking nor the classification of the various industries is the same in the two cases.

Since these figures represent broad industrial groups, the averages cover a wide spread in each case, and they tell more about the relative position of different industries than about the comparative rewards attached to different kinds of work. But they have a significant influence in wage negotiations, inasmuch as the spokesmen for various industrial groups tend to attach increasing importance to the place of their own members in what has come to be known as the 'league table' of earnings, with the result (of which more later) that every group which slips back scrambles to regain its place. For years printers and workers engaged in vehicle production have maintained their position at or near the top, while workers in the distributive trades and farm workers remain stuck near the bottom. Yet what, one may ask, are the peculiarities of printing which account for its persistently elevated position? Is it particularly skilled or responsible or arduous or dangerous or of exceptional national importance as compared with, say, mining, or working on the land?

In the occupational, as distinct from the industrial, tables both non-manual and manual workers are included together, and no surprise will therefore be occasioned by the facts that the spread is wider than in any of the tables already quoted, or that the managerial group headed the list (in April 1973)[1], with gross weekly earnings of £91.8, while general farm workers stood at the bottom with £25.3. Actually the agricultural group includes five categories of which only the foremen passed the £30 mark at £31.7. Scattered between these extremes

1. Latest figures available: *Department of Employment Gazette,* January 1974.

were scores of other occupational groups such as administrative and executive civil servants at an average of £65.6, production and works managers at £54.2, crane drivers at £42.1, firemen at £40.2, shop assistants at £32.5, general labourers at £32.3 and caretakers at £28.8. Printers were not separately shown, so it is not possible to compare their occupational with their industrial ranking, but they certainly were (and are) among the better paid manual workers. In general the pattern is familiar, if not universally acceptable – the more agreeable and interesting jobs being in the upper ranges, while those that are less attractive (though not always less necessary) are down below.

Against these official averages it may be illuminating to set some individual examples drawn from a remarkable investigation undertaken in 1972 by Robert Lacey for the *Sunday Times*[1] into the take-home pay (after payment of income tax and other deductions) of nearly 50 wage-earning and salaried persons. This was based on data said to have been either supplied by the subjects themselves, or extracted from publicly available records. Top of this list was her Majesty the Queen whose net official pay (as distinct from her private income, the size of which is a well-kept secret) was reckoned at £5,769 weekly. Next came the Chief Executive of the Green Shield Trading Stamp Company, who began his working life as a laundry boy and was said to be 'by far Britain's highest paid executive' with a gross salary of £260,000 a year at age 54, plus dividends on shares in the company, making in all a net weekly pay packet of £1,313 (though he was said to be 'entitled to earn more'). Beside this, the Archbishop of Canterbury's net weekly pay of only £106 (plus subsidised accommodation) looks modest enough – but not as compared with Eric Roberts, a Barnsley miner, age

1. *Sunday Times* Magazine, 1 October 1972.

42, who worked underground for 5 days a week from 6 a.m. to 1.15 p.m. (without a lunch break) for £24 weekly (and even for that he had to thank the 1972 miners' strike), plus about 9 tons of free coal annually. Meanwhile Roberts' ultimate boss, Derek Ezra, Chairman of the Coal Board, at 53 was taking home £192 each week (also recently raised, but without the necessity of striking). In Birmingham Robert Morris, a constable of 24, netted only £29, while, at 62, William Weems, an assistant rodent officer in Westminster, had to make do with £26, and Christine Woodward, 27, a ballet dancer in the Convent Garden Royal Corps de Ballet, received £24 net for 41 hours' work, not counting time spent in dressing up and practice before each performance; but she was supplied with three new pairs of tights each year, and four or five pairs of ballet shoes every week. But of all the people in this collection the two lowest paid were Cecil Burton, 56, a Norfolk farm worker (who also held a certificate as a Craftsman for Machine Operation and Maintenance) with £17 for a week's work, and Marilyn Rookyard, aged 18, earning £13 a week at Woolworths, supplemented by meals in a subsidised canteen, a Christmas bonus of £13.89 and a day off on her birthday.

It seems improbable that this picture (along with nearly 40 other cases, not quoted here) will appeal to anybody as completely 'fair'. The *Sunday Times* did not follow up its investigation by a systematic survey of public reaction to it, and the few surveys that have been undertaken have generally covered only a relatively narrow spectrum of occupations within the wage-earning field as ordinarily so-called. However, for what they are worth, the results of these have been generally critical of things as they are. Thus in January 1973 the 'Working Together Campaign' published the results of a national survey carried out by National Opinion Polls Market Research Ltd. on the public's views on 'the present share-out of wages between all the different jobs' in Britain.[1] Of those questioned 46% categorised the existing distribution as 'unfair' and another 22% as 'very unfair', while it was regarded as 'fair' by only 17% and 'very fair' by a mere 2%. (The remaining 13% expressed no opinion.) Thus over two-thirds of the respondents rejected the notion that existing wage relativities corresponded to their personal conceptions of fairness. Asked to rank 12 named occupations in the order of what these should in their opinion be paid, the respondents produced a list which did not correspond at all closely to the rating of these jobs in respect of actual earnings, as the following table shows.

| Rank according to valuation by public | | Rank by actual average gross earnings in a standard week | |
|---|---|---|---|
| 1. | Underground miner | 1. | Docker |
| 2. | Ambulance driver | 2. | Car production worker |
| 3. | Maintenance craftsman | 3. | Maintenance craftsman |
| 4. | Heavy goods vehicle driver | 4. | Heavy goods vehicle driver |
| 5. | Farm worker | 5. | Miner |
| 6. | Bricklayer | 6. | Railway guard |
| 7. | Docker | 7. | Bus conductor |
| 8. | Car production worker | 8. | Ambulance driver |
| 9. | Refuse collector | 9. | Bricklayer |
| 10. | Railway guard | 10. | Refuse collector |
| 11. | Bus conductor | 11. | Factory cleaner |
| 12. | Factory cleaner | 12. | Farm worker |

Other similar investigations (as for example in the BBC *Man at Work* series) have also shown valuations by members of the public which differ markedly from the pay actually earned in various occupations. Such composite pictures no doubt generally conceal wide differences of individual opinions, but divergent

1. The date of the actual survey is not mentioned in the Report but as any of the official statistics of earnings quoted relate to 1971, it was presumably 1971 or 1972.

views may nevertheless have a negative, if not a positive value, inasmuch as they suggest that the existing picture does not command general approval. The most significant feature of the 'Working Together' enquiry was the very high proportion of those questioned who consider the distribution of wage incomes as unfair or very unfair.

This curious pattern of wages and salaries can only be explained as the historical deposit of both economic and social forces, the latter having been long underestimated in traditional economic theory. Not so long ago economists claimed that, whatever the structure of wages might be, it was what it was as the result of the operation of inexorable economic laws which were beyond human control. Ricardo's doctrine that 'Labour like all other things which are purchased and sold and which may be increased or diminished in quantity has its natural and its market price' (originally enunciated shortly after the end of the Napoleonic wars) has indeed had a long life. It lingered on into my own student days in the first world war when I was enjoined to study a work[1] the purpose of which was, in its author's words, 'to show that the distribution of the income of society is controlled by a natural law'. So inexorable indeed was that 'natural law' in the opinion of some nineteenth-century economists that the pressure of trade unions was said to be wholly ineffectual and incapable of having any effect on the wages actually received by their members. Supply and demand dictated that wages would be high in occupations where labour was scarce, and *vice versa*; and, since people are presumably reluctant to enter jobs which

1. Professor J.B. Clark's *Distribution of Wealth*, published some eighty years after Ricardo's pronouncement. As Professor Robert Lekachman has since observed in his *History of Economic Thought* (Harper Bros., New York, p.285) Clark's argument carried the corollary that 'competitive distribution was not only efficient . . . but also equitable'.

involve dirt, discomfort, or danger, it followed that these would tend to be better paid than those which are clean, safe and agreeable. (This, too, I was taught as a student, in flat contradiction to everyday experience.)

Such theories are hardly borne out by the *Sunday Times* survey; nor indeed by the official occupational statistics. The fact that the Archbishop of Canterbury's net weekly wage packet (exclusive of the subsidy on his accommodation) is 6 times as large as that of a farm worker is not due to any shortage of Archbishops or to the necessity of attracting more recruits to this office by the prospect of better pay. It is farm workers, not Archbishops, who are in short supply. Many indeed of the curiosities which I noticed twenty years ago survive to-day in defiance of classical economic theory — among them, the anomalous position of professional football players, whose remuneration I then found difficult to reconcile with the doctrine that every wage 'tends to be equal to the "marginal net product" of the labour for which it is paid'. Football wages have certainly risen dramatically in twenty years, and the £34,000 fee which I quoted as the possible transfer fee for a 'star' performer looks ridiculous beside to-day's quarter of a million: also a player does now receive, as of right, a modest proportion of the sums for which he is bought and sold. But if the transfer fee represents his true market price, why do the laws of economics not enable, or even compel, him to extract the whole sum from his employers? Why the difference between the footballer and the pop-singer?

The validity of economic theories about wages has in fact always rested on implicit assumptions about the social structure, the very strength of which is indicated by the fact that it is so seldom thought necessary to spell them out. No doubt if all choices were open, workers would normally prefer pleasant and safe employments to those that are disagreeable and dangerous, and would only be willing to enter the latter if they offered exceptionally good wages. But all choices are not and never have been open. Even while the economists have been elaborating their theories in academic seclusion from the realities of industrial life, social factors have been influencing the pattern of wages and salaries even more powerfully than have economic laws. Supply and demand have accommodated themselves to rigid social conventions rather than *vice versa,* and it was (and is) the pleasanter occupation which carries the higher pay. Nor do fringe benefits compensate for differences in wages. On the contrary they too conform to the same social pattern: the higher the pay, the longer are the holidays, the better the canteen, the more generous the sick pay and the pension. Even the language commonly used is governed by respect for the established social hierarchy: no one refers to the 'wages' of the Lord Chief Justice or (as yet) the 'salaries' of the miners.

Nevertheless times are changing. Recently the influence of social conventions on comparative pay has been challenged from two quarters. First, in certain areas, ironically often those in which trade union organisation is relatively weak (as, for example, the pay of part-time domestic cleaners), market forces have begun to behave as the textbooks say they should behave, and scarcity of labour has had a direct effect in pushing wages up. Second, the growing, but unevenly distributed, power of trade unions has endowed existing relativities with a new sanctity, since keeping one's place in the 'league table' has become one of the most popular arguments for increased wages. As the Pay Board's Report on Relativities observed: 'Collective bargaining as it is practised in this country has no mechanism for making enduring changes in the relative pay of groups in separate negotiating units'.[1]

1. Cmnd 5535 of 1974, p.5.

These challenges, however, still meet with powerful resistance from the established order. The influence of purely economic factors operates mainly (Mr. Clive Jenkins and his professional workers notwithstanding) within a limited area of industrial wages as ordinarily so-called. Over a wider spectrum, from the top salary to the lowest wage, social factors still play the predominant part in shaping the pattern of incomes. If here and there a bricklayer earns £100 a week, this still occasions the raising of eyebrows amongst persons much more highly remunerated. But the established conventions stand their ground. In July 1973 the Review Body[1] on Top Salaries, after one brief paragraph of argument, concluded that the maximum individual increase of £250 p.a. permitted by the (then operative) Stage 2 ought to be awarded to everyone covered by its terms of reference, that is to say, to persons in receipt of salaries ranging from £8,250 to £27,500; and at the same time the analogous Body[2], which periodically reviews doctors' and dentists' remuneration, recommended that top consultants' salaries should be raised from £7,350 to £7,599 p.a.

Who can be surprised that the picture resulting from this combination of social stratification, smash-and-grab and the attempts of individuals to make the best of the often very limited opportunities open to them, should fail to evoke general enthusiasm? But we can at least congratulate ourselves that both social conventions and smash-and-grab, unlike the supposedly inexorable laws predicated by classical economists, are the products of human volition and therefore controllable. (Who now believes that wages cannot be affected by trade union activity?)[3] Never-

1. Review Body on Top Salaries, *Second Interim Report on Top Salaries,* Cmnd. 5372 of 1973.
2. Review Body on Doctors' and Dentists' Remuneration, *Third Report,* Cmnd. 5353 of 1973.
3. But a similar belief in the autonomy of price movements dies hard. See pp.

theless the dilemma is inescapable. Either we must live for ever with the anomalies of our present wage structure, or we must incorporate into our incomes policy some criterion of fairness by which an equitable relation between work performed and remuneration received can be established.

In terms of IGT this implies that the primary grading, which is intended to soften contrasts of affluence and poverty, must be modified by a secondary graduation allowing larger tax-free increases of income to groups of workers who can establish that they are paid less than the nature of their work justifies. Fairness therefore must again be defined — not, as previously, in relation to the overall pattern of income distribution, but in the narrower context of the relativities between particular classes of workers; and once again the definition must be expressed in terms of concrete criteria capable of being applied in practice. Without such criteria the adjective 'fair', even in Edward Heath's speeches, is as irrelevant and as meaningless as other less reputable four-letter words in current usage.

In the search for these criteria, the first step must be to emancipate ourselves from the astonishingly widespread belief that 'fair' decisions can spring fully-fledged from the heads of 'impartial' persons acting as arbitrators. This belief, which has long bedevilled industrial relations, certainly dies hard. In the introduction to its first Report the PIB proudly claimed to be such an 'independent and impartial agency', no doubt recalling that the Royal Sign Manual by which it had been established had referred to the 'desirability . . . of ensuring that the benefits of faster growth are distributed in a way that satisfies the claims of social need and justics'; but at least the PIB, unlike the typical arbitrator, had definite terms of reference (embodied in the schedules to the 1966 Act) to work to. Again and again in wage disputes the parties are exhorted to have recourse to 'impartial' arbitration. In the acrimonious railway dispute of 1973-4, an arbitrator was waiting in the wings, and the railwaymen were repeatedly blamed for their reluctance to avail themselves of his services and repeatedly also reminded that his 'impartiality' was above suspicion. Again, when the 1974 miners' dispute was referred to the Pay Board we were constantly assured of the Board's unique 'impartiality'. Yet without any disrespect to its members, it must be recorded that they were certainly not well-known public figures, nor is information about their relevant experience and qualifications readily accessible. Of the seven original members only the Chairman, who had formerly been Director-General of the National Development Office, and one of his colleagues who had had extensive experience in banking, rated an entry in the 1973 *Who's Who*.[1] Nevertheless it was widely assumed that the inherent impartiality of these generally unknown six men and one woman, with the addition of the (recently retired) Chairman of Fisons and the former Secretary-General of the Staff Side of the Civil Service National Whitley Council, was a sufficient guarantee that they would be able to find fair terms of settlement of an exceptionally contentious and economically dangerous dispute.

This naive faith in impartiality is also responsible for the not uncommon practice of inviting members of the judiciary to arbitrate in industrial disputes on the ground that they are, by profession, impeccably impartial. Again it is no disrespect to our learned judges or to their virtues to point out that their functions in the courts and as industrial arbitrators are radically different, and that their impartiality in the former is no qualification for the latter.

1. I understand, however, that between them the other members could claim considerable experience in the field of personnel management.

Obviously anyone involved in settling questions of
pay must be impartial in the elementary sense that he
does not approach the matter with a determination to
give as much as possible to one side or the other. But
without law, precedent or established principle to
refer to, fairness has no meaning, and in relation to
wage claims no such standards exist to which
particular issues can be referred. Only in the interpretation of existing agreements can arbitration be a
judicial process comparable to procedure in the
courts. In the courts, in a civil case the judge, having
heard the evidence of the disputants, decides whether
one party has libelled the other or broken a contract
or done him any other wrong which is recognised as
such by law. In a criminal case he instructs the jury
on the law relating to the offence with which the
accused is charged, and tries to guide them in
assessing whether the evidence in the case does or
does not establish the defendant's guilt. In each case
his impartiality is demonstrated by his application of
the law to the facts as presented, without the faintest
bias towards one side or the other. But where there is
no law there can be no impartiality in its application.
Indeed the one good reason for employing judges to
settle industrial disputes is not that they are impartial, but that many of them are very clever men – so
clever that they may even devise solutions which
persuade everybody concerned that he has won, as
Lord Wilberforce did in the Electricity Supply
dispute of 1971. But such decisions have nothing to
do with 'social justice' or 'fairness'. Even a judge
cannot be impartial in a vacuum.

The prevalence of the contrary view has had some
curious consequences. First (as I have personally
experienced from some years' service on the Civil
Service Arbitration Tribunal) the evidence submitted
to arbitrators tends to be curiously irrelevant. Thus,
evidence about changes that have occurred in the

relative positions of different grades or groups can only be evaluated if it has already been decided how far differentials and relativities are sacrosanct. To the arbitrator who holds that they are, it is a straight-forward business to decide in the light of evidence whether they have, or have not, been disturbed. But what if his colleague is equally convinced that the whole object of the exercise should be to adjust existing relativities as being, in his opinion, inequit-able? Who is to judge between these opposing views? Each argues with equal impartiality from different premises. But without guidance as to which premises are relevant, no rationally defensible decision is possible, and whatever the evidence submitted, this cannot contribute to the emergence of an 'impartial', or objective, judgment.

Second, faced with this dilemma arbitrators may either attempt to assess the justice or injustice of the claims on which they have to decide by their personal standards of equity, or they may try to apply standards that they believe to be generally acceptable. (In this situation the happiest arbitrators are obviously those who have persuaded themselves that this is not a real choice at all, because the world thinks as they do; and the unhappiest are those whose conception of equitable wages differs most radically from the present standards of payment.)

Third, arbitrators (even if they happen to be judges) may tacitly jettison any idea that they must apply principle or law to the issues before them, and try instead to find some compromise which all parties to the dispute will accept, without troubling their heads about its 'justice' or 'injustice' at all. In such cases they come very near to accepting that ultimately the only relevant law is the law of the jungle — smash-and-grab.

It is therefore greatly to be hoped that if and when the Industrial Conciliation and Arbitration Tribunal jointly proposed by the 1974 Labour government and the TUC materializes, the myth of the impartial arbitrator will no longer be perpetuated, and that explicit criteria for the 'fair' settlement of wage disputes will be prescribed. Certainly that myth can give no help in the selection of cases for specially generous tax-free increases under IGT's secondary grading, or for any other form of exceptional treatment. Principles must be explicitly formulated for the guidance of whatever authority is responsible for identifying these cases; and because these principles, like those which govern the initial grading of IGT, inevitably embody subjective social valuations they must be the subject of political discussion and decision, and not be left to 'experts'. Both the PIB and the Pay Board had in turn to grapple with this problem of defining special cases, and the lessons of their experience should provide a basis on to which to build the structure of IGT's secondary grading – or indeed any alternative system designed for the same purpose.

In the case of the PIB definite terms of reference were prescribed by Act of Parliament; and these, together with the Board's reactions to them, have already been discussed on pp.40. To this story the Pay Board subsequently added a further substantial chapter, which began in March 1973 when the government asked for advice on the question of the 'wider relativities' raised by groups which from 'time to time feel that they deserve special treatment in order, for example, to improve their relative position within the community or in relation to other parts of the same industry'. The Board's Report on this subject was requested for the end of the year, no doubt with a view to leisurely consideration in the drafting of a Stage 4 at some remote future date. In November, however, the miners began an overtime ban in support of their claim to increases in pay outside the limits of Stage 3. Since wider relativities were obviously the crucial issue in this dispute, the Board's considered suggestions on them might have been expected to be highly relevant to the search for a settlement. Nevertheless neither the Board nor the government showed the slightest sense of urgency. On 13 December, when the miners' overtime ban had already been in force for a full month, the Chairman of the Board told the Secretary of State, who was said 'naturally' to accept the position, 'that we ought to take a little more time'.[1] There was apparently (and not surprisingly) much evidence to be considered, but if the government felt any impatience at this attitude, not a hint of this ever reached the public.

Eventually, however, on 24 January 1974 the Report was published. It was immediately seized upon by the government, the Opposition, the TUC and the mineworkers' leaders, who proceeded to engage in a game of musical chairs by alternately hailing it as a miraculous solution to the dispute in the mining industry, and rejecting its findings as irrelevant to the immediate crisis. But the Report's authors (who had counselled caution and practised what they preached on every page) had already expressed the view that its proposals would work most effectively if they were not applied to 'cases put forward in a situation of crisis'.

Actually the Report did not advance matters very far. A useful distinction was drawn between 'differentials', as meaning the pay differences within a single negotiating group, and 'relativities', defined as relationships between the pay of jobs in different pay negotiating units — irrespective of whether those units operated in different plants under different employers or in different sections of the business of a single employer. But on the problem of making sense of

1. *Incomes Data Services,* Report 175, December 1973.

relativities as thus defined, the Report was deeply pessimistic. The nature of this problem was found to be 'such that there is at present no technique to hand of general application, no single formula or criterion for determining whether pay relativities are right in terms of economic or social factors, and no ready means of diagnosing trouble in advance'. The conclusion is indisputably true, but nevertheless relativities in the Board's own words 'are the main standard by which employees judge the fairness of their own pay' – and some attempt had, and has, to be made to rationalise them.

In the end therefore the authors of the Report did commit themselves to what they described as the 'formidable' task of devising a plan for dealing with relativity problems. This was to be a four-stage procedure. First, the Secretary of State, usually after advice from the CBI and the TUC, would make a preliminary selection of cases for 'further examination for eligibility for special treatment'. The wording is not entirely clear, but suggests that the Secretary of State would be able to veto applications right at the outset, so that those which he rejected would go no further. The Report did however add that 'there would probably need to be a statement of guiding principles and procedures for the selection process', also to be worked out in conjunction with the CBI and the TUC. Yet must not the government originally have hoped, when they asked for advice about the problem of 'objectively considering' claims for special consideration, that the Board would itself give some indication of what those guiding principles might be? But on that the Report went no further than a suggestion that 'possible tests' for the selection of special cases might include 'a statistical criterion for earnings increases well below the average',[1] and 'a major change in the

1. Although the authors were alive to the fact that 'if everyone below the average had an increase equal to the average, the average would of course be different and higher'.

function of relative importance of an industry or a major reorganisation of a service'. In addition, it was suggested that 'in due course new criteria (e.g. ones relating to low pay and manpower shortage) might need to be added', and that 'the Secretary of State should also be free to select other cases for consideration on grounds of national interest'.

Those who succeeded in passing this first hurdle of selection by the Secretary of State would then be subject to 'examination in depth and in public' 'by or on behalf of an examining authority'. Again the question of the precise criteria to which this authority should refer was evaded. Instead, account was to be taken 'of a wide range of interests, particularly those of related groups', and 'all relevant economic and social factors' would be examined. In order to ensure consistency and coherence the Report further suggested that the Board might itself be given this task; but since this would involve 'a considerable widening of its role, the impact . . . on its composition would need to be considered'.

After all this, a recommendation would be made to the Secretary of State on the special treatment, if any required; and finally the Pay Code would be appropriately amended so that the Secretary of State could issue a specific recommendation providing for an increase beyond the prescribed pay limit.

This procedure would obviously involve considerable duplication between the Secretary of State's selection and the subsequent 'examination in depth', and would therefore necessarily operate very slowly. Applicants would have to clear three fences – the Secretary of State, the examining authority, and (so far as the survivors of these two stages were concerned) the Secretary of State again. But this could hardly fail to result in the examining authority going over much the same ground 'in depth and in public' as the Secretary of State had already covered in discussions with the CBI and the TUC about his preliminary selection — unless of course different criteria were employed at each stage, in which case only confusion could result.

These proposals were, however, quickly overtaken by events. On 8 February 1974, only just over two weeks after the publication of the Relativities Report, Parliament was dissolved and the government, reversing its previously dilatory attitude and ignoring the Pay Board's plea that relativities should not be examined in a state of crisis, referred the question of the 'Relative Pay of Mineworkers' to the Board, with a request for a full Report to be produced 'as urgently as is consistent with thorough examination of all the interests and factors involved'; and for this purpose the Board's membership was strengthened by the two additions already mentioned, who, if not widely known to the public, had at least both had relevant experience, one as an industrialist and the other as a trade union negotiator.

The outgoing government immediately expressed its readiness to accept in advance the findings of the Board, which in its new discretionary role was now freely endowed with the virtue of untarnishable impartiality. Indeed it began to look almost as if the issue in the ensuing election campaign was not, as frequently suggested, whether the democratically elected government or the unions should govern the country, but whether the government had not in fact abdicated in favour of the (to the general public nameless and faceless) members of the Pay Board who were now entrusted with absolute authority to settle the issue which had led to the dissolution of Parliament.

The Board tackled its task with an unaccustomed sense of urgency and its Report was duly published on 6 March 1974. At its first public hearing the Chairman is reported to have claimed that the occasion was 'without precedent' and that it had 'introduced a new idea into the process of wage determination'. The Board was said to be 'taking part in a unique experiment'[1]; and in due course the Report itself endorsed these assertions by a declaration that its authors had made it clear that their 'task was not to act as a court of inquiry, an arbitration tribunal or a conciliation hearing'.[2]

All this was no doubt good public relations. But had it any more solid foundation? Like the typical arbitration tribunal or court of enquiry the Board had to proceed without any guidance as to the standard by which it should judge what was 'fair', and was thus in the position of a court which was required in the course of its proceedings to write the statutes that were to be applied to the cases in hand. Under its terms of reference, the Board was merely instructed that it should take into account 'not only the case of the mineworkers but also the position of others who would be affected by improvement of the mineworkers' relative position' and that its examination should 'also cover all the economic and social factors relevant to the case, including the continuing need to reduce the rate of inflation'. Even these instructions, however, were treated somewhat lightly, no doubt because, as the Report modestly put it, the 'circumstances were not ideal': the investigation had to be conducted in a tearing hurry, and in the very situation of crisis which the Board had already indicated as an unfavourable climate for any such operations. Not surprisingly, therefore, no reference was made to inflation; nor did the Report's recommendations, which came within an ace of awarding the miners all that they had asked for, suggest that its authors had this topic much in mind. As for external

1. *The Times*, 19 February 1974.
2. Pay Board, Report on the *Relative pay of mineworkers*, Cmnd 5567 of 1974, p.2.

relativities with other industries, the Board reported
that it had been hampered by 'conflicting statistical
evidence' in its attempt to 'demonstrate the movements in earnings in coalmining as compared with
other industries', and it could therefore only conclude in general terms that 'the relative position of
coalmining *vis a vis* manufacturing industry' had
'changed considerably over the years' and that the
gain resulting from the Wilberforce Inquiry in 1972
had 'since been eroded'. Apart from those observations, the Report hardly went beyond the conclusion
that 'if exceptional treatment were given to all those
employed by the NCB there would be repercussions',
as there certainly would – and were. British Rail, the
Electricity Council and the Gas Corporation had all
given warnings of what was likely to follow; and
British Rail in particular showed no intention of
letting the grass grow between its rails. Already on 21
February a railway spokesman had given evidence to
the effect that 'the changed social and economic
environment, together with the manpower shortage
and relatively low pay' created 'an irresistible case for
the railways to be given special treatment'; and,
although no formal relationship had been established
between surface workers in the coal industry and
railway employees distributing coal from the pit
heads, there was nevertheless said to be 'a strong
informal relationship' between the two groups.[1]

The two factors to which the Report did pay
particular attention were, first, the urgency of reversing the drift of men away from the mines in view of
the increased importance of the coal industry consequent upon the dramatic increase in the price of oil;
and, second, the nature of a miner's work, especially
in respect of the dangers that it involves to life and
health. On the first of these issues the Board drew
the conclusion from statistics of the recent loss of

1. *The Times,* 22 February 1974.

manpower from the mines that it was going to be difficult even to maintain output at current levels, let alone to achieve the increased production that now seemed likely to be required. The relation of these losses to wage levels and movements in the mining industry or elsewhere was not, however, discussed; nor was there any sign that the Pay Board either shared, or could dispel, the uneasiness about the efficiency of what might be called the carrot method of directing workers from one job to another which had caused the PIB to sheer away from this subject altogether.

In the Report's analysis of the nature of a miner's work, there were again echoes of the 1966 directives to the PIB, notably to the clause which allowed claims to exceptional treatment where the pay of a group of workers had fallen seriously out of line with that of others doing 'similar' work. Inevitably any such provision must raise the question of how 'similarity' should be defined. But here the Pay Board was, in a sense, on an easy wicket, at least so far as underground workers were concerned. Since miners are the only people who habitually work underground, and since, moreover, no other industry involves comparable risks of both ill-health and accident, the Board could neglect this problem with a clear conscience. Comparable employments, it argued, simply did not exist, nor had any of those who gave evidence claimed a direct pay link with underground workers which might have disturbed this conclusion. It was therefore sufficient to establish that miners working underground ought to be 'well paid'. What this might mean in relation to the wages of, say, workers on the car assembly lines, or printers setting up national newspapers or young women secretaries could be left for others to interpret.

The plain truth is that the Pay Board's investigation, like the Wilberforce Inquiry[1] of two years

1. Cmnd 4903 of 1972.

earlier was inexorably conditioned by the political and psychological climate in which it was conducted. It would have been politically unthinkable that, in February 1974 in the heat of the election campaign, any Court, Tribunal or Board should have reached the conclusion that the miners were not entitled to anything above the Stage 3 limits – and the possibilities of wangling something extra within those limits had already been exhaustively explored without success. On the other hand, it would have been highly impolitic to give the miners quite all that they had demanded. The Board therefore, following both the arbitrators' traditional canon and the Wilberforce precedent, came up with a recommendation that far exceeded anything compatible with Stage 3 but just fell short of the miners' original claims.

The lessons to be drawn from this story, and from the previous experience of both the PIB and its successor, as to the criteria by which cases should be selected for special exemption under IGT secondary grading, are both positive and negative. On the negative side the Pay Board (unlike the PIB) having been given no principles to work to, was obliged to argue from premises of its own choosing in order to justify the conclusion which it was in fact predestined to reach. But those premises (though never explicitly formulated) may well have set a useful precedent for the future. Paradoxically, neither the Report on Relativities, nor that on the relative pay of mine-workers, gave any great weight to 'relativities' as enshrined in the league table of earnings. A significant hint was thus dropped that claims to special treatment cannot be justified *merely* on account of a loss of rank in the table.

Such claims are indeed objectionable on three grounds. First, as things now stand, the fact that certain groups of workers earn approximately similar pay gives absolutely no support to the inference that they must be engaged in work that is in any sense similar: the links are fortuitous and irrational. Second, attempts to perpetuate the pattern of relative earnings as established at any given moment must produce a structural rigidity wholly incompatible with a dynamic economy in which new industries and new methods continually supersede others that have become outmoded. Third, since any increase in pay that is designed only to restore the claimants' position in the table will inevitably trigger off a host of consequential claims from other groups on similar grounds, the total effect is bound to be a highly inflationary process of 'leap-frogging'.

Loss of status in the table of comparative earnings should not, therefore, be included among the criteria by which special exemptions from IGT might be justified, and claims based solely on this ground should not be acceptable. Indeed in future the less heard of the league table, the better. In any case, insofar as the primary IGT grading favoured the lower incomes, the table would be liable to major disturbance from this factor alone, and that in itself should deal a death-blow to the sanctity with which some negotiators seek to invest it.

Of the categories which the PIB was enjoined to consider as exceptional cases, two would appear to be unsuitable for IGT special exemption. These are, first, those cases in which workers have made a direct contribution to productivity, and, second, those in which pay is too low to provide a reasonable standard of living. Claims for increases under productivity agreements would certainly raise important questions, but they can hardly be regarded as 'special cases'. In principle productivity or payment by result schemes are closely akin to overtime, inasmuch as they result in higher pay to those who work longer, or more productively. Moreover, although in certain types of work they would be impracticable, they are scattered widely over a variety of occupations and industries. It would therefore be more logical to include them (if they are to be recognised at all) with other possible sources of additional income which might be *generally* disregarded in assessments of IGT liability, rather than to treat them as special cases — just as voluntary overtime and certain other increments of income were treated as outside the pay limit under Stages 2 and 3 of the 1973-4 counter-inflation policy.[1]

Second, the exclusion of low pay from the special case procedure under IGT would be justified so long as the primary IGT grading (as here proposed) allowed higher tax-free increases in the case of all low-income groups. If, however, this did not adequately cover every case in which earnings failed to provide a reasonable living standard, the appropriate remedy would be to revise the primary IGT grading, not to extend the scope of 'special cases'.

On the other hand a good case can — in theory at least — be made for writing into the criteria for IGT special exemptions the two remaining categories to which the PIB was instructed to give special consideration under the 1966 Act — namely cases in which a redistribution of manpower was required in the national interest and in which it was likely that this could be effected by a revision of wage rates. The difficulties here, and the reluctance of the PIB to admit this criterion have already been mentioned. Since this Board's demise, Mr. Aubrey Jones[2] has endorsed its hesitations. The imperfections of the labour market, the difficulty of establishing that increases in pay in any given instance are an effective influence upon labour mobility, and the danger that an increase designed to pull one way will be negatived by counter-increases pulling in the opposite direction

1. These and other such general disregards are discussed in the Chapter that follows.
2. *The New Inflation* (Penguin Books, 1973) p.78.

have all led him to find 'the conclusion inescapable' — that 'an exception to the "norm" on the ground that it is necessary to provide incentives for an improved distribution of manpower – is better omitted'. On the other hand the views of the Pay Board[1] were, at least at first, somewhat tentative. While agreeing that, where there is a general shortage of labour, it is counter-productive to allow firms to bid against one another, the Relativities Report argued that 'some weight' might be given to 'the manpower situation of an industry' in considering the selection of special cases, although this should not be used as a 'conclusive criterion'. When, however, less than a month later the Board was called upon to consider the miners' pay claim, the tune was changed and the manpower situation became the predominant theme in its argument for conceding an exceptional increase.

Shortage of labour is an argument freely used by trade unions claiming higher pay; and it is no less certain that this argument is often based merely upon figures of the number of persons leaving an industry within a given period, and that it is not precisely related to prevailing rates of pay, or to sophisticated calculations as to the volume of employment which is desirable in the national interest either in the field which the workers are deserting or in that to which they are migrating. Indeed this is one of the commonest examples of the often irrelevant arguments which unions are apt to plead in support of claims which they are really advancing on quite different grounds.

Nevertheless, I do not think that we can uncompromisingly slam the door in the face of these economic factors as a claim to special treatment. As the official figures regularly show, the public services in particular constantly rank low in their rates of pay, and they are also constantly plagued by shortages of staff. In 1973 the Post Office threatened

1. Pay Board Report on Relativities, p.12.

to cut off second daily deliveries of mail because of a shortage of postmen (a threat which was later carried into effect in rural areas but officially justified at the time on grounds of scarcity, not of postmen, but of fuel). Recently also the Civil Service has come to rely upon temporary typists supplied by commercial agencies (an arrangement which is neither efficient nor economical), apparently because the rates paid to clerical grades in the Service do not produce sufficient recruits. In face of the scores of other such examples which come to light day after day and, above all, in view of the prominence that the Pay Board gave to this factor in its Report on mineworkers' pay, it is difficult to go the whole way on this issue with Aubrey Jones' views, as stated in early 1973.

Shortage of labour should therefore be acceptable as a possible ground for special IGT exemption, but only if supported by much more thorough investigations than have generally been undertaken when the subject has hitherto been raised in relation to wage settlements.[1] In particular, as already suggested, claims on this ground should be backed up by the best possible estimates of not only the immediate, but also the longer term, manpower demands of the deserted industry; by accurate information as to comparative earnings in the deserted and in the receiving industries; and by sample surveys of the reasons given for their change of employment by the workers themselves. It is certainly not enough just to assume either that adjustments of pay in an industry which is losing its workers will of themselves produce the distribution of manpower thought to be 'desirable in the national interest', or that they may not be dangerously inflationary. Aubrey Jones' warnings

1. But in view of the pressure under which it had to work the Pay Board cannot be blamed for not having examined the subject in depth in its Report on miners' pay.

should always be kept in mind, even if it is not always possible to accept his conclusion. Perhaps the appropriate model is to be found in the words of the 1966 White Paper on the Period of Severe Restraint[1] which took the view that pay increases on grounds of manpower shortage could only be justified subject to 'the closest scrutiny in the national interest'; and added the salutary admonition that 'where there is a shortage of labour to undertake essential work, every effort must be made to meet the shortage by a more effective use of the manpower available'.

Finally, disregard of status in the league table emphatically does *not* mean disregard of relativities as between persons employed on genuinely similar work. Indeed it should not be overlooked that it was 'similar', not 'comparable', work which the PIB was instructed to use as a criterion in identifying pay that was out of line — a formula which clearly excluded purely conventional links in the pay of particular groups. The league table would no doubt be relevant, if in fact its ranking was based on similarity of work or on any attempt at a rational assessment of differences; but as a compound of smash-and-grab, social prejudices and economic pressures it can have no claim to embody any rational principle. On the other hand, the rule that people engaged in genuinely similar work should earn about the same pay is probably more widely accepted than any other principle commonly invoked in wage negotiations, and should certainly be an acceptable ground for special treatment in appropriate cases.

Similar pay for similar work is, however, only a first step. If, as the Pay Board had to admit, 'relativities are the main standard by which employees judge the fairness of their own pay'[2], it will be necessary to face the much more difficult task of

1. Cmnd 3150 of 1966.
2. Report on Relativities, p.3.

rationalising the relationship between the wages earned for *dissimilar* work. This means that attempts must be made to extend and refine 'job evaluation' procedures. Since all such evaluations inevitably involve comparisons of unlike with unlike it is illusory to suppose that they ever can be wholly objective: in the nature of the case they must be based upon arbitrary principles. Nevertheless arbitrary principles consistently applied may well give more acceptable results than decisions which pay no respect to either principle or consistency; and, as the Pay Board has drily commented, at present the choice of comparisons in wage negotiations is made as best suits the positions of the two sides, since 'collective bargaining does not usually place any premium on consistency in argument'.[1] In circumstances in which the correctness of an answer cannot in the nature of the case be proved or disproved, the virtues of consistency are not to be despised.

Job evaluation schemes have been more widely applied abroad than in this country but it is noteworthy that both the PIB and the Pay Board made encouraging noises about its possibilities. In two valuable Reports[2] surveying job evaluation techniques and schemes both at home and abroad the PIB certainly gave a hint that this was the area in which the solution to its own problems might eventually be found. But at the time of these enquiries (December 1968) only four British cases were identified in which industry-wide job evaluation was in operation in a full sense: these were coal-mining, jute, cotton-spinning and doubling, and the Scottish woven wire industry. However, a considerable number of individual firms had schemes of their own, and the Board estimated that in a survey covering nearly 6½ million workers about 23% had

1. Report on Relativities, pp.5, 6.
2. PIB *Report on Job Evaluation* (Nos. 83 and 83 (Supplement).)

their pay grade determined by job evaluation, and that, if all the companies then contemplating the introduction of such schemes were to go ahead with them, this proportion would rise to about a third within the next few years.

These PIB Reports also examined a number of schemes tried out in other countries, notably in the USA, Sweden, West Germany and Holland. On the whole the scope of these has been narrow, and their influence conservative rather than revolutionary, although shortly after the war the Dutch introduced a scheme which was said to be applicable to all manual workers. Some of the American and Swedish experiments have been designed on more ambitious lines, assigning points for such diverse factors as skill, effort, responsibility, and working conditions or hazards. These have, however, not escaped criticism for a tendency to give a noticeably higher rating to skill and responsibility as compared with effort and working conditions — perhaps, one may suspect, because job evaluations are generally drafted by persons who have had more personal experience of the burdens of skill or responsibility than of danger and discomfort, and are, therefore, tempted to overweight the former in their valuations of the factors that should determine pay.

Subsequently the Pay Board in its turn added an Appendix on Job Evaluation to its Relativities Report, recording that there had been a 'substantial increase in the number of employees covered by job evaluation schemes' since the PIB's investigations, and that the Board had studied a small number of schemes covering workers in more than one employing organisation. These, it was suggested, might well be extended with advantage to other industries, although scepticism was expressed about ambitious proposals such as those submitted in evidence by the Institute of Personnel Management which would 'cross the boundaries of different establishments and sectors of the economy' and 'could lead to the acceptance of general yardsticks for establishing pay relativities between a wide range of jobs'.

Job evaluation is a large and complex subject and all that can be said here is that it is urgently necessary to press on with the development of increasingly sophisticated analyses which will provide the basis for more rational evaluations of various types of work, and thus make possible the establishment of criteria by which the claims of particular occupations and industries to special treatment could be assessed at least with some degree of consistency. Obviously this is a task which must be tackled jointly by both sides in industry, so that these criteria may be acceptable as well as consistent; and, since it is bound to be a task of great complexity, and liable also to meet resistance from powerful vested interests and violent prejudices, much patience will be necessary. But in the end this is the only road that can lead to an alternative to smash-and-grab.

To sum up in the light of this discussion. We now have a programme which includes an IGT, imposing 100% tax on the excess over a prescribed increase in purely personal income, regardless of the source from which that income comes. In the first instance this tax is to be levied at levels graduated (primary grading) according to the size of the taxpayer's net income remaining after payment of income tax, more substantial increases being allowed on smaller than on larger net incomes. This graduation would, however, be subject to modification (by secondary grading) in cases concerning employed (or self-employed) persons, in which one or other of the two following conditions was satisfied: first, that they were in receipt of lower pay than others engaged on generally similar work, or were earning less than they would be entitled to by the valuation of their work in accordance with some accepted procedure; or, second, that it was necessary in the national interest to attract further recruits to the occupation or industry concerned by the prospect of higher wages. Claims based on purely traditional linkages or on any *a priori* assumption that the claimants are entitled to retain whatever position in the table of earnings they may have previously occupied would be inadmissible.

Of these two permitted grounds for exceptional treatment the first would be justifiable primarily as a matter of equity, the second by economic necessity. In practice the two might sometimes point to opposite conclusions. (The Pay Board's recommendations about the miners, which, it will be remembered, were based on these — albeit unexpressed — premises, succeeded in avoiding conflict between them insofar as the conditions of underground mineworkers were found to be unique.) In general, however, it would seem that equitable considerations should normally enjoy priority, but that these might have to be over-ridden where there was good reason to believe that a serious shortage of manpower could not be remedied without a more substantial increase in pay than would otherwise be justified; and 'good' reason as already suggested would have to mean much more than what now passes for 'evidence' on this issue.

For deciding claims to special IGT exemption it would be necessary to establish a Board which, in order to differentiate it from the PIB, the Pay Board and the abortive Relativities Board, I shall call the IGT Special Exemptions Board or SEB. In many respects this would be a reincarnation of the old PIB, at least insofar as that body's functions related to pay. Like the PIB, the SEB would make recommendations in accordance with explicit instructions as to the grounds on which special exemptions would be permissible, and would therefore enjoy much wider discretion than the Pay Board (until its brief reincarnation as the Relativities Board), but without being required, like the 'impartial' arbitrator, to arrive at 'fair' decisions in a vacuum. With the establishment of the SEB, the Pay Board would, of course, be left to rest in peace.

It is hardly necessary to emphasise the desirability of the SEB's membership being drawn from the ranks of employers and trade unions, together with representatives of the general public of consumers. The fact that IGT would affect *all* incomes, great or small, falling with increased severity on the well-to-do, should mitigate the hostility that the unions felt to the 1973 Pay Board, and induce them to accept representation; but if they continued adamant, their absence would not be fatal. In any case the Board's task would be of a technical nature. Even if an element of subjective judgment inevitably entered into its interpretation of the prescribed conditions, it would, like the PIB, but with far wider discretion than the Pay Board, be engaged, not in making the rules, but in seeing that they were correctly applied. Should, however, the SEB have the misfortune to be boycotted by the unions, it would still be essential that it should be composed of persons who not only have had relevant experience, but can also command wide public respect.

Whether the SEB should also include governmental representatives would depend upon whether its decisions required Ministerial confirmation, in which case both government and civil servants should be excluded (as in the case of the PIB) on the ground that government would have the last word anyhow. Although Ministerial confirmation would be bound to mean delay (and heaven forbid that wage decisions should be deferred as planning decisions are!), it would seem preferable to include this requirement, since its omission would leave too much power in the hands of a body not directly responsible to the electorate.

To these proposals there are one or two corollaries to be added. The preferential treatment of the lower paid under the primary IGT grading would not only, as already mentioned, undermine the sanctity of existing relativities; it would also tend to lighten the burden of claims that would come before the SEB. Insofar as the low-paid would already be getting more generous increases in income than those above them, the incentive to demand special treatment would be weakened. The task of the SEB, which would deal only with exceptional claims, would, therefore, be far less quantitatively formidable than that of the Pay Board, which between 2 April and 30 November 1973 handled 7804 settlements covering nearly 18 million employees under Stage 2, as well as another 257 settlements under Stage 3 involving an additional 2 million employees. Most of these cases can hardly have had more than a routine examination. But if the SEB would have far fewer to deal with, it would certainly have to think harder about each of them.

The PIB could only examine cases referred by government; and the Relativities Report proposed that the preliminary selection of 'special' cases should be made by the Secretary of State, preferably with advice from the TUC and the CBI. Both these procedures seem inappropriate for the SEB as being unduly restrictive. On the other hand it would, I think, be equally inappropriate for the Board to allow itself to be cluttered up with claims from individuals that their personal work is in some way 'special'[1] or that they have been assigned to the wrong occupational classification. The function of the SEB would be to deal with factors affecting, not individuals, but particular occupations or industries which might justify these being classified in an exceptional category. Applications should therefore only be accepted

1. The procedure for dealing with individual grievances is discussed in the Chapter that follows.

for consideration if they came from organisations representing workers or employers in such occupations or industries, or, alternatively, from the Secretary of State in cases where he thinks that the national interest is involved (as for example in the distribution of manpower).

The actual procedure of the Board, it is earnestly to be hoped, would be both speedy and informal. The PIB set a good precedent here. Eschewing both the paraphernalia of formal legal procedures and of public hearings, it worked through formal and informal interviews with the parties concerned as well as direct investigations — often both confidential and extensive — of its own. In its Reports on particular settlements (as distinct from more general studies) it generally worked to a three months' time limit. By contrast, the Pay Board's Relativities Report, with its proposal that a preliminary selection procedure (which would itself presumably take some time) should be followed by 'examination in depth and in public' which would look into 'all relevant economic and social factors' showed a characteristic absence of any sense of urgency, such as the SEB, failing some dramatic change in the industrial climate, would be unlikely to be in a position to afford.

Finally the SEB would have to know where it stood financially. The primary grading of IGT should be so arranged as not to absorb the whole of the funds available for increases in incomes, a margin being left expressly to cover the special cases approved by the SEB and accepted by government. The amount of this margin would be included in the budget estimates and therefore subject to the usual Parliamentary scrutiny; but, since the necessary calculations would not be easy to make, it would be desirable that the SEB should be periodically provided with revised estimates of the rate at which its recommendations were eating into the total assigned for special exemptions. It could then be in a position to tailor its recommendations accordingly.

# VI

## Incomes Gains Tax:
## Some Loose Ends

THE CLAIMS OF groups of workers to special treatment on account of the nature of their work discussed in the preceding chapter would undoubtedly be much the most formidable complication that would have to be woven into the fabric of IGT; but there are still some loose ends. Most of these relate to the question whether there are any increases of income, derived from wages, salaries, profits, dividends or anything else which ought to be disregarded in assessing liability for IGT.

Some of the candidates for exemption are covered by the Pay Codes' rules about who could overstep the pay limit, and these may in certain cases be applicable also to IGT. Regular increases under previously agreed incremental scales were exempt from the pay limit under Stages 2 and 3, and there can, I think, be no argument against following a similar course in relation to IGT. If, moreover, this should have the incidental result of encouraging the spread of such scales beyond the limited range of professional and white-collar occupations in which they are generally found, and should lead to their more general application to the wages of manual workers, this would be a development greatly to be welcomed. At present wage-earners, especially those paid by the week, customarily reach their maximum wage at the age of 18 or 21 and remain fixed there till retirement. But there is no reason why this should be so. Although it is true that the weekly-paid are on the whole likely to change jobs more frequently than their salaried professional or managerial colleagues, nevertheless it is well established that when any of the latter do move to new employments, they are, by negotiation, placed at an appropriate place on the scale, and do not automatically have to start again at the bottom. It should not be too difficult to introduce similar arrangements into a much wider range of occupations; and this would have the great merit of enabling an employee to look forward to a rising income without the risk of aggravating inflation; since, as the elderly and more highly paid workers retire or die and are replaced by those who are younger and less expensive, nothing is added to the total wage bill.

As at present constituted, however, many scales are open to the objection that they are spread over too many years, and that the increments are badly spaced in relation to the normal pattern of personal expenditure. The expensive period in family life is the time when there are young children at home — the more so to-day when women frequently continue in paid employment after marriage, but may have to give this up while producing and rearing a family. In consequence, with the present trend to early marriage, family income may only reach its peak under a long drawn-out scale at the point when expenses are beginning to decline. There is therefore a case for shortening scales which are spread over fifteen or twenty years. Indeed it might be logical for increments to diminish towards the end of a scale, thus obviating the risk that, if maximum rates are reached earlier and therefore payable for a longer period, the total wage bill would be increased, with inflationary consequences. But, with or without such modifications, it is much to be hoped that the use of incremental scales will be greatly extended into the wage-earning field, the increments provided being automatically exempt from IGT.

Similarly, increases due to a change of employment

or to promotion must also be exempt from IGT liability, again following the analogy of the Pay Codes' practice in relation to the pay limit. But here a word of caution may be advisable. Experience under the Codes has suggested that a watchful eye needs to be kept to ensure that these changes are genuine, and not fictitious devices for securing additional pay.

Overtime raises slightly more complex issues. First, it must be appreciated that even if no allowances at all were made under IGT for the exemption of overtime earnings, this would be no discouragement to overtime working as such: IGT would merely diminish the incentive to undertake *additional* overtime over and above what had been previously worked. Thus, if a worker's average weekly pay in 1974 amounted to £45 including £5 overtime, and at this level he was entitled to, say, a 10% increase of income in 1975, he could earn another £4.50 by still further overtime without the IGT axe falling on this, provided only that there had been no change in his basic rate. IGT would do no more than set an eventual limit to the amount of overtime that could profitably be worked. Since there are obvious physical (and indeed social) limits to the hours that anyone can or should work, the disincentive effect of IGT in this context would be unlikely to be serious, even if no exemption was allowed for overtime earnings as such.

To allow no such exemption might, however, bear hardly on any worker who, not having previously worked overtime, subsequently wished to do so. Also, a distinction must be drawn between 'contractual' overtime which an employee is required to work under his terms of employment, and 'voluntary' overtime which he undertakes at his own option. The Stage 2 and 3 Codes included the former within the pay limit but exempted the latter, so long as there was no alteration in the ratio between basic pay and overtime rates. In the case of IGT probably the simplest course would be to retain this arrangement in principle, but to disregard voluntary overtime only up to a certain maximum, which could be expressed either as a percentage of the basic wage earned or as a total of permissible hours. The allowable percentage increase on the IGT scale would then be calculated on the total of the basic wage plus contractual overtime plus any earnings from voluntary overtime up to this maximum. Thus anyone with an IGT grading of 10% would be able to increase his income by overtime up to 10% of this total, but no more in any given year. In this way an employee could undertake a moderate amount of voluntary overtime without fear that the tax collector would snatch the rewards from him, whether or no this was a new departure on his part or had been his habitual practice in the past.

More tricky problems arise in connection with possible IGT exemptions for increased pay resulting from productivity schemes. 'Productivity' in this connection has had a dubious history and is almost a dirty word. It is indeed common knowledge that in the past some productivity agreements have, in the words of Hugh Clegg, been 'wholly spurious'. Moreover, in view of the contemporary tendency to conclude such agreements at a shop-floor level, it is exceedingly difficult to keep any effective overall check upon whether they are or are not genuine. In the White Paper of April 1965[1] which was reproduced in the 1966 Act, the relevant formula used was fairly restrictive. Higher pay above the current norm could only be allowed if, for example, employees had by 'more exacting work' or by 'a major change in working practice' made a 'direct contribution' to the productivity of the firm or industry concerned; and even then it was prescribed that 'some of the benefit should accrue to the

1. Cmnd 2639 of 1965.

INCOMES POLICY: AN INQUEST AND A PROPOSAL

community as a whole in the form of lower prices'.

The Pay Codes have also been tough on this subject. Stage 2 allowed only payments under schemes already in operation or agreed before November 6, 1972; but Stage 3 had to face the more difficult problem of how to deal with new productivity schemes that might be introduced in the future. The solution adopted was to allow additional pay earned under such schemes to be exempt from the pay limit only if restrictive conditions elaborate enough to occupy an entire page of the Code were satisfied in full. These included provisos that the net savings arising from a scheme must be 'sufficient to reduce unit total costs and unit labour costs below the level they would be but for the introduction of the scheme': that the excess above the pay limit must not be more than 50%: that the Pay Board must be notified in advance of the details of the scheme; and that no increase in pay must be paid before the net savings contemplated had been actually realised. And so on. During the first month of Stage 3's operation fourteen proposals for new efficiency payment schemes were reviewed. Details of the results of these examinations were not, however, included in the Board's Third Report, covering the period up to the end of November 1973, no doubt because there had not been time to make all the enquiries necessary to establish whether all the requisite conditions (of which those quoted above are but a modest fraction) had been complied with. Indeed one wonders whether it would ever be possible for the Board to satisfy itself on this matter unless inspectors were appointed to conduct on the spot minute and continuous examinations of every case submitted.

In face of these complexities, there would seem to be only two alternatives in relation to IGT. The first would be to copy the conditions applicable to productivity agreements under the Stage 3 Code, and to allow any payments which could squeeze through this fine mesh to escape IGT. The second would be to forget about productivity schemes altogether, and to treat any additional earnings from these in the same way as any other wage increase: that is to say, to provide that, in calculating whether any individual's income has increased up to the limit at which IGT becomes payable, these payments must be included. Personally I would opt for this last course, on the following grounds: first, the Stage 3 test would be almost impossible to apply with demonstrable accuracy, if only because in most productivity schemes the respective contributions of workers and management are likely to be inextricably intermingled; second, since it would be only on fairly substantial incomes that IGT would impose an absolute standstill, most workers would in fact retain a proportion of the rewards of any special contributions they might have made under productivity schemes; and third, there is good sense in the doctrine of the 1966 Act that 'some of the benefit of increased productivity should accrue to the community as a whole'.

Certain other categories of income also demand special consideration. The first is the position of the self-employed worker running his own business. Suppose he opens up a new branch or otherwise extends the scale of his operations – what then? As previously explained, the Pay Codes were concerned, not with a business man's personal income, but with the limitation of the profits of his business expressed as a percentage of sales or turnover, to the so-called 'reference level' (normally the average of the best two of the preceding five years); but special provisions were also included which modified this 'reference level' in cases of 'a substantial reconstruction of the enterprise' or a 'substantial change in the character of its business'. IGT, however, is essentially a personal tax, imposed only on money that gets into someone's pocket or personal bank balance, and nothing but confusion could result from imposing it on business profits as such, as distinct from the income of the proprietor of a business. At the same time there are obvious objections to putting obstacles in the way of the owner of a successful business who wishes to use his profits in opening a new shop or branch establishment. It would therefore seem appropriate to allow exemption from IGT for additional income which has definitely been used by the owner in a substantial reconstruction or a substantial change in the character of his business.

Related issues arise also in connection with the treatment of the profits of corporate enterprises. Logically the arguments for retaining the essentially personal nature of IGT require that it should not be levied on corporate profits as such. This conclusion is moreover supported by the fact that to impose the tax on these profits would in a sense involve double taxation, since distributed profits would be subject to IGT when they were paid over to shareholders. Nor would companies be able to deduct IGT from dividends, as is customary with income tax, because they would be unaware of the financial circumstances, and therefore of the IGT liability, of their individual shareholders, just as they are similarly unable to deduct surtax or the higher income tax rates by which surtax has been succeeded.

It is to be hoped, therefore, that in this matter logic — and the surtax analogy — would prevail, and that no attempt would be made to impose IGT on corporate profits. If, however, on the face of it this proposal looks politically unacceptable, there are other weapons in the armoury. Corporation Profits Tax, to which company profits are already subject, is an appropriate instrument for mopping up excess profits; and although it is difficult to be very optimistic about the efficiency of price control[1], it is to be hoped that the preventive influence of IGT on excessive profits would be far from negligible.

A further analogy can be drawn between the successful business man who ploughs his profits back into his business and any other individual who makes a remunerative investment out of income. Personal saving has been regarded as a virtuous activity ever since the days of Queen Victoria; and even to-day, although the unconditional quality of this virtue has been somewhat tarnished by the writings of the late Lord Keynes, saving is generally regarded as laudable if it results in genuinely new investment and a consequent addition to total national output. But the practical difficulties of distinguishing between genuine and fictitious saving, and between genuine and fictitious investment, are formidable indeed. Genuine saving and genuine investment emphatically need to carry the warning: Beware of imitations! Judicious rearrangement of a portfolio of shares may result in both capital gains and additional income. But such transactions do not add a single nut or bolt to the national output, even though they produce additional income. In principle therefore such increases in income have no title to escape the net of IGT.

However, the practical difficulties of distinguishing the genuine from the fictitious in this context are so great that it would probably be necessary to abandon any attempt to make any such differentiation under IGT. After all, IGT falls upon any excess over the permitted exemption which a worker can get for his work. Why should additional income derived from extra work be treated less favourably than that produced by personal thrift? In the end therefore it may be the most equitable as well as the most practicable course to treat any addition to investment

1. See pp. 165 ff.

income, whether due to higher dividends, rearrangement of investment or new savings out of income, as all alike subject to IGT.

Still other sources remain from which personal income can be increased. One can win money on the pools or by other forms of betting, or one can receive gifts or inherit income-yielding assets. All of these are non-inflationary, inasmuch as they are merely transfers from one person or group of people to another. In previous statutory incomes policies they have therefore been ignored. Under IGT the proceeds of betting and gifts could without question be treated in the same way, if only on the ground that few of us make substantial incomes from these sources. On the other hand bequests (together with gifts taxed as bequests because they have occurred within the period before the donor's death which renders them liable to estate duty) constitute a more substantial item, and on the face of it there might seem to be a case for bringing newly inherited income under IGT, as part of a long-term policy for controlling income distribution. However, having considered various methods of achieving this, I have become convinced that they would all involve glaring anomalies, and that additions to income from inheritance should therefore be exempted from IGT in the same way as successful bets or gifts. Inasmuch as bequests do not aggravate inflation, there is no cause for concern on that score, and any undesirable effect which they may have on the overall distribution of income would be more appropriately dealt with by revision of the system of death duties.

The above discussion relates only to the income from bequests, as distinct from the capital from which this income is derived. This raises the important question of the relation between IGT and the present Capital Gains Tax.

143

In drawing the line between capital and income there is always an area of indeterminacy. To most people a house is a capital asset, and indeed many house-owners never own more than one in their whole lives. Others who move around more frequently may buy and sell two or three. But in contrast with these unmistakably capital transactions, there are people who make a living out of regularly buying and selling houses or other property. Obviously it would be quite wrong if IGT could be dodged in cases where a regular income is derived from dealings in what in other contexts would be regarded as capital assets. The logic of treating the proceeds of such transactions as income, and not as capital gains, was indeed admitted even by a Conservative Chancellor of the Exchequer. In his final mini-budget of December 1973 Mr. Anthony Barber claimed that profits from speculation in land were already taxed as income, and outlined new measures for dealing with landowners who can, as he said, 'quite fortuitously make huge windfall gains simply as a result of decisions made by planning authorities acting on behalf of the community as a whole'.[1] The sentiments were admirable, but the practical measures proposed were hedged about with restrictions the effect of which would be to confine their application to very substantial transactions. Moreover, speculative gains are not confined to dealings in land: equity no less emphatically requires that anyone who increases his income by speculating in the foreign exchange markets or in produce such as wheat, copper or zinc, should be just as much subject to tax as a speculator in land values. All such incomes would therefore be liable to IGT; and it would be for the Inland Revenue authorities, who are well accustomed to differentiating between capital gains and income, to apply that distinction in such a way as to leave no suspicion

1. House of Commons Hansard, 17 December 1973, col. 957.

that any income escaped IGT by masquerading as a capital gain.

In order, however, to make assurance doubly sure, there may also be a case for revising the present method of charging Capital Gains Tax. Of all the ways of adding to one's wealth, a capital gain owes least to the recipient's own efforts. At best he can claim to have made a prudent investment, but thereafter he is continuously enriched as he eats, sleeps and goes about his business—as a well-to-do landowner and progressive farmer once sadly observed in my hearing, when he estimated that in the 1970-72 Stock Exchange boom he could have made more money by just sitting on his bottom waiting for his shares to rise than he ever realised from his extensive farming activities. Such capital gains are at present (May 1974) liable to tax at a flat rate of 30% irrespective of the owner's wealth or income, subject to a proviso which allows part of the gain to be taxed as investment income. If, however, the rate of tax were graduated on a scale that rose in relation to the taxpayer's total capital, the incentive to pass off increases in income as capital gains could be effectively diminished.

Two other cases perhaps call for special treatment. The first is that of the person whose income drops because he has had a spell of unemployment or of sickness. Suppose that in 1974 a man who was fully employed was in receipt of a net income of £2,000, and that at that level his IGT exemption rate was 10%. In 1975 he would normally be able to earn up to £2,200 without incurring liability to IGT, but it might happen that as the result of a spell of unemployment or sickness his income actually dropped to £1,500 in 1974. If by 1975 he had quite recovered, then, unless some special provision was made, he would be limited for that year to a maximum income of £1,650 (£1,500 + 10%). In these circumstances it would seem fair that he should have the right to claim that his permitted increase in 1975 should be calculated by reference to his 1973, instead of 1974 earnings. Since, however, no tax system can be expected to give total protection against all the ills that man is heir to, this concession should be confined to cases where loss of income was due to sickness or unemployment. Other misfortunes such as a decline in trade in the case of a privately owned business, or a reduction of income on retirement, would be ineligible; but if the drop was very severe, there might be some compensation resulting from the fact that at a much lower income level, a more generous IGT grading would be applicable, allowing, say, a maximum increase of 20% instead of only 10%.

Secondly the position of juveniles may be regarded as anomalous. In the statistics relating to the distribution of earnings many of the very small figures at the bottom of the tables refer to the wages of juveniles. Any IGT grading, therefore, which allowed higher exemptions on the smaller incomes would allow juveniles to move up the scale relatively rapidly, although it does not necessarily follow that under their terms of employment they would in fact be paid up to the limit that would be free of IGT. If, however, this is thought to confer an undue advantage upon the young worker, it would be a simple matter to fix a specially reduced rate of IGT exemption for all persons under 18.

The outline IGT that I have sketched is only an outline. In the actual drafting of a scheme the taxation experts will no doubt be quick to discover many other practical problems and questions to be decided; and these they must be left to grapple with. I would only emphasise that my outline is only one of many possible variants; and that it is also one of the simplest. I have for example assumed that tax would be charged at 100% at the point at which it

146

became operative; but if this is unpalatable, it would be perfectly possible to substitute a graduated rate so that earlier increments of income were chargeable at a lower rate, and the 100% level only reached after a considerable increase in income had been attained. This would in effect mean a double graduation for everybody subject to IGT, the rates of tax chargeable being (a) determined by the level of the taxpayer's previous income (as I have proposed) and (b) rising on successive 'slices' of any addition to this.

Personally I would prefer the simpler 100% rate for three reasons. First, it would be a way of applying to all personal incomes a restriction which previous policies applied only to earnings. Under the Stage 2 and Stage 3 Codes every worker was absolutely restricted to the pay limit. For practical purposes this was equivalent to 100% tax on anything over and above what this formula allowed; but (notwithstanding the restrictions on business profits and dividends) no comparable limitation was imposed upon the additions to their incomes which individuals could (and did) make in other ways. The formula was therefore grossly discriminatory against the working population, and trade union resentment on that account is both understandable and justified. Second, an absolute limit is obviously a better protection against inflation than an elastic one: a sliding scale would certainly add to the difficulties of calculating what rates of IGT exemption were consistent with the growth of available output. Third, in the contemporary scene, simplicity deserves to rank as a virtue in itself. Among the more unattractive features of modern capitalist societies are their ever-increasing complexities. These not only result in rules that are often unintelligible to those affected by them (as, for example, the multiplicity of means tests and the maze of regulations governing entitlement to social security benefits), but sometimes also place formidable obstacles in the way of quite modest changes.[1] It must therefore again be emphasised that it is the principle of IGT, rather than any particular grading, that is important, and that my particular proposals can easily be modified by those who find them either insufficiently · or excessively equalitarian. But the innovator should always keep in mind the maxim: when in doubt choose the simplest patterns.

To complete the picture I now add a few examples of how IGT might in practice work out in individual cases; but it must be clearly understood that these are hypothetical illustrations suggesting increases beyond what would be practicable, not only in the dismal economic climate of early 1974 when these words are written, but also, all too probably, at the time when they appear in print. Moreover, if and when fairly substantial increases do become possible, the value of money will probably have changed so much that it may appear incredible that anybody could be earning less than £1,000 a year. (As a hint of what might happen, it may be salutary to recall that less than twenty years ago £1,000 was the salary of a professor, in the University of London: whereas in April 1973 a bus driver's average earnings amounted to over twice that figure.) But IGT is intended as a long-term policy, and it is not unreasonable to hope that rates of increase on the scale shown might be feasible in the foreseeable future. On the other hand, changes in the value of money are so unpredictable that it seems best to quote levels of income that do not look too unrealistic at the moment. In any case, however, the

1. For example: In 1973 when the Misuse of Drugs Act came into force, repealing its predecessors the Dangerous Drugs Acts and Drugs (Prevention of Misuse) Act, it seemed reasonable on the face of it that statutory instruments issued under the 1973 Act should be listed under the letter 'M' instead of under 'D'. Such, however, was the havoc which this simple change would apparently have wrought in the Stationery Office's indexes that it was rejected as impracticable.

object of these examples is merely to illustrate the method in which IGT would be applied — and for this purpose it is immaterial what precise figures are used either for specimen incomes or for IGT grading.

Subject to these reservations, IGT scales are assumed to allow —

20% IGT-free increases on net incomes up to £1,000[1]
10% on net incomes from £1,001 to £3,000
5% on net incomes from £3,001 to £4,000
2½% on net incomes from £4,001 to £5,000
nil on net incomes above £5,000

## Examples

(1) Miss Smith is a secretary earning £1,200 p.a. in 1974 after income tax and has no other source of income. Her maximum IGT-free income for 1975 at the 10% exemption rate would be £1,320. She could therefore get a rise in salary of up to £120 in 1975 without becoming liable to IGT.

(2) Mrs. Brown is a pensioner with an income from National Insurance and her former employers amounting together to £800 in 1974, and she also receives £200 from various investments, giving her a total income of £1,000. Her permitted maximum income for 1975 is thus (at the 20% exemption rate) £1,200. However in 1975 her investments did very well and her income from that source rose by 50% to £300, although her pension was not increased; but even so, at a total of £1,100 she would be £100 below liability for IGT. Alternatively if, in addition to her increased dividends, her pension was raised by 10%, her total income would reach £1,180, so she

1. In all the examples and illustrations given, incomes are expressed in round figures. In practice, since 'income', for IGT purposes means income after deduction of income tax and other statutory deductions, it is unlikely that this actual take home (or take-bank) pay would be in such round figures. This I have ignored so as to simplify calculations, and give a clearer picture.

would still be £40 below tax liability. She could, in fact, enjoy a 12½% rise in her pension before the IGT axe would descend.

(3) Not so Mr. Snooks. Mr. Snooks is also retired, but with a pension of £2,000 p.a. Like Mrs. Brown he receives in addition dividends from investments, amounting in his case to £400 p.a. which gives him a total income in 1974 of £2,400. His permitted maximum (with 10% exemption) is therefore £2,400 + 240 = £2,640. If his pension is unchanged, but his dividends, like Mrs. Brown's, have risen by 50% to £600 his actual income in 1975 will be £2,600 leaving him still £40 below the IGT level. If, however, his pension, again like Mrs. Brown's, has been increased by even as little as 5%, his 1975 income will be £2,100 + 600 = £2,700. He will therefore have to pay £60 of this to IGT.

(4) Mr. Miller is a factory worker. From his basic weekly wage in 1974 he took home £40; and he did no overtime. On this basis in 1975 his permitted maximum (at a 10% exemption rate) would be £44, and his union has succeeded in getting this for him. However, there has been an addition to his family, and he does not think that the extra £4 will be enough. He would therefore like to work some overtime. If a limited amount of overtime is dis-regarded under IGT, it will pay him to work up to that limit, which, as already suggested, might be calculated either as a proportion of his basic wage, or as a fixed number of hours. In the former case, supposing this proportion to be fixed at one-fifth of the basic wage, Mr. Miller could increase his weekly pay from £44 by £8.80p giving him a total of £52.80 without liability to IGT. Alternatively, if a total of 5 hours additional overtime was the maximum exemp-tion, then, assuming a normal working week of 40 hours and overtime at time and a half, his hourly

rates would be £1.10 per normal working hour and £1.65 for each hour of overtime. In that case with 5 hours' overtime he could raise his weekly pay from £44 to £52.25.

(5) Mr. Parker is a street cleaner earning £25 per week or £1,300 p.a. in 1974 at which level his normal IGT exemption rate would be 10%, allowing him a tax-free increase of £2.50 which would bring his 1975 pay up to £27.50. His union has, however, made a successful claim that the work of street cleaners is currently undervalued and that they should be entitled to a 15% IGT-free increase. He can therefore earn up to £28.75 in 1975 without incurring IGT liability.

(6) Sir Lancelot Silverspoon holds an important public position for which he received £11,000 a year after payment of income tax (equivalent to a gross salary of about £25,000). Any additional income above that will be wholly absorbed by IGT.

# The Case for an
# Incomes Gains Tax

I HOPE THAT enough has now been said to establish that IGT is in principle a viable policy; but every attempt to control inflation by any kind of fiscal device is certain to meet instant criticism. Thus the Liberal Party's proposal during the February 1974 Election campaign to introduce an anti-inflation tax on increases in prices, wages or dividends above a prescribed norm provoked the *Times*[1] to comment that 'it is not a new idea'; while the *Financial Times*[2] observed that 'The attractions of using fiscal means to curb inflationary price and wage increases have long been recognised, but the idea has always foundered on the practical problems of implementation.'

The *Times* (which then proceeded to dismiss the project in somewhat contemptuous terms) was quite right. The idea was not new: it had for example been the basis of a proposal advanced by myself in the *Listener*[2] nearly three years before, and in occasional articles even earlier. Now, perhaps, it is not too much to hope that the amplification in this book may have gone some way towards solving the practical problems recognised by the *Financial Times,* without destroying the admitted attractions of a fiscal incomes policy.

One favourite criticism is that any proposal to work an incomes policy through the tax system would involve a monstrous proliferation of bureaucracy. For this the Liberal Party's proposal was a ready target, and its publication was followed by

1. 13 February 1974
2. 1 April 1971.

hysterical outbursts in some newspapers. 'How many civil servants' cried the *Daily Telegraph*[1] 'would be needed for such minute regulation of everyone's income?', while the *Daily Mirror*[1] prophesied that 'like other deceptively simple schemes', the proposal 'might well turn out a bureaucratic nightmare. Every pay-roll would have to be combed'.

The Liberal scheme was undoubtedly much more complicated than that put forward in this book. It was designed to operate a combined incomes and prices policy through a single tax, which in its structure and proposed method of administration, as well as in its treatment of investment income, differed in principle from my IGT scheme. Nevertheless one can but wonder whether the authors of the comments just quoted had studied either the clause of the Stage 3 Code relating to productivity agreements which I have partially summarized on p.139, or the criteria by which the Price Commission is required to judge whether the price charged for some article or service is excessive — or whether indeed they had ever so much as glanced at the Code at all. If they would peruse these documents, they would observe the appalling complexity of the system set up under the Counter-Inflation Acts; and it is against this that any new project must be judged. And can it be that those who paint alarmist pictures of civil servants 'minutely regulating everyone's income' had never heard (or even had dealings with?) the Department of Inland Revenue whose officers are paid, day in, day out, to do just that?

Actually it is one of the strongest arguments in favour of IGT that control of incomes would be operated through the Inland Revenue authorities. After a taxpayer's liability for income tax had been calculated, an additional assessment would be made of any further sum due for IGT, both being paid in

1. 13 February 1974.

153

the same way. Complaints by the taxpayer would then fall into two classes. First, he might object to his assessment as having not taken proper account of his personal circumstances, claiming, for example, that an increase in his income was consequent upon promotion, or was an agreed annual increment. Decisions on such questions are not far removed from those that Inland Revenue officers have constantly to make as to what may properly be included under business expenses; and they would certainly involve no more fiddling detail than, say, the claims that some university teachers have been known to submit for depreciation allowances on their academic gowns (some of which, from their appearance, a layman might be forgiven for supposing to have already been written down to zero). Such claims would in the first instance be dealt with by the local Tax Inspector who would already be conversant with the claimant's affairs. Should, however, the Inspector's decision be unacceptable to the taxpayer, an appeal should lie, as in other tax disputes, to the General or Special Commissioners of Income Tax. In reaching their decisions both the local tax officers and the Commissioners would be guided by definitions of what should automatically rank as payments exempt from IGT (as for example agreed annual increments); and these definitions, many of which might be taken over from the Pay Codes, would be written into the formal structure of the tax itself, either by statutory instrument, or possibly as a schedule to the Act by which it was established. In this way, through machinery already established all over the country coverage would be complete, as it could never have been under the Pay Board, since the Board was more than fully occupied in reviewing settlements in order to ensure that they were consistent with the Codes; and it is hardly conceivable that a centralised body sitting in London could have kept an effectively watchful eye upon everyone up and down the country who claimed to have changed his job or to have been promoted — from which one suspects that rumours about 'phoney promotions' and the like may have been not without foundation.

The second class of appeals would come, not from individual taxpayers, but from organisations claiming that their members' work was currently undervalued, and that they should be entitled, under the provision for special cases already proposed, to tax-free increases larger than those normally applicable to persons in their income bracket. These claims would be referred, as described in Chapter V, to the SEB, which would also consider similar references from the Secretary of State in cases in which he thought that exceptional exemptions from IGT were necessary in the national interest. Apart, however, from these claims, there would no longer be any need for the review of settlements which was the major function of the Pay Board under the Counter-Inflation Acts.

Equally disposable might also be the 'Review Bodies' which advise the government about the remuneration of doctors and dentists in the health service, and about 'top salaries'. Under IGT a considerable proportion of the personnel with which these bodies are concerned would be likely to be earning too much to be eligible in the foreseeable future for any IGT exemption (i.e. for any increase in salary) at all, so there would be nothing for these bodies to do. Their very creation, moreover, was originally a concession to the social prestige of persons considered too grand for their remuneration to be settled in the same way as that of more proletarian callings; but from the day that the pay limits under the Counter-Inflation Codes became applicable at all levels, that consideration ceased to be relevant. These specialist bodies are, moreover, open to the further objection that their staff cannot have the experience and expertise that would be gained in the service of a Board covering a wider range of incomes. The introduction of a fiscal system of controlling incomes might therefore have the effect of still further simplifying procedure by the abolition of this monument to snobbery.

Another easy stick with which to beat IGT is the suggestion that it would be damaging to incentive. This, however, ignores the fact that, insofar as the effective working of our economic system depends upon the response of individuals to financial incentives, *all* incomes policies, without exception, must be suspect on this account. Every such policy must by definition to some extent dull the edge of financial incentives. The effective choice, therefore, is between no policy at all and a policy which, by depriving people of income that they might otherwise have enjoyed, nevertheless may in some degree discourage their efforts to work harder or more productively; and the real issue is whether IGT would be more damaging to incentives than alternative policies. This challenge, I submit, it can meet reasonably well. So far as the working population generally is concerned, IGT would allow for a steady rise in income with preference to the low-paid, and it would not penalise overtime as previously worked plus the extra hours allowed as exempt. It must again be emphasised that it is not overtime, but ever-increasing *additional* overtime which the tax would catch. It would therefore in principle be no more destructive of incentives than the Stages 2 and 3 formulas which also set absolute limits[1] to any increase in a worker's pay, but which were nevertheless curiously free from criticism for their destructive influence upon incentives. Whether IGT would in practice be more or less drastic than the Stage 3

1. Apart from increases from threshold agreements, voluntary overtime, or profit-sharing.

formula would of course depend upon its graduation.

At the top of the scale, however, where no increase of net income is permissible, financial incentives would admittedly disappear. But again IGT would be only marginally more severe than the Stage 3 Code, under which no one (apart from the glaring exceptions permitted by the profit-sharing clause) might earn more than an additional £350 gross p.a., or just under £7 a week; and IGT notwithstanding, it would still be open to a high-ranking salary-earner to improve his position by moving to another even better-paid post, if such were available. If, however, he had already reached the ceiling for IGT exemption and saw no better prospect elswhere, is it seriously suggested that, say, a member of the Board of a nationalised industry or a top civil servant or a medical consultant would neglect his duties because an ungrateful government had failed to hand him a few extra heavily taxable thousands every year or two? Moreover at these exalted levels, insofar as incentives operate at all, they tend to be comparative rather than absolute: it is the sight of other people advancing more rapidly than oneself which has a peculiarly inflammatory effect. But since IGT would impose the same restrictions on everybody in the same income bracket, this passion would not be ignited. Well-paid people certainly like to *talk* about the damaging effect of heavy taxation upon their own and their colleagues' performance, but where is the evidence that their deeds support their words?

In this connection I cannot refrain from reference to the radical theory propounded by Dr. Jeffrey Gray[1] of Nuffield College and the Department of Experimental Psychology at Oxford in the highly respectable columns of the *Times*. Writing primarily on the subject of the genetic element in intelligence, Dr. Gray argues against the common assumption that

1. 8 September 1972.

those who have superior ability must receive extra rewards because otherwise they would not use this as society needs. If intelligence is largely determined by heredity, it cannot, he says, be true that, in the absence of differential rewards, fewer people would be willing to undertake jobs demanding high intelligence, since no financial inducements can produce superior brains that nature has failed to provide. Differential rewards would only be necessary if highly intelligent persons would actually prefer to do work that required only a low level of intelligence, and would therefore have to be persuaded to the contrary by the prospect of extra money. But that proposition, adds Dr. Gray, is not even plausible: 'How many engineers would choose to work on the assembly line if only the pay was the same?' So perhaps after all the classical economists (with Dr. Gray's encouragement) will have the last laugh.

Finally it is sometimes argued that the counter-inflationary effect of IGT could be more simply produced by reducing the amount of money in circulation through tighter credit control. To this criticism there are, I think, two answers. The first hinges on the fact that the purpose of IGT is not merely to contain inflation. It has another, and a no less important, objective, namely, to modify the distribution of income; and, since it is graduated by reference to the personal income of individuals, its effects on distribution can be calculated and adjusted to produce whatever pattern is politically deemed to be equitable. By contrast, the effects of a deflationary monetary policy upon personal income are untraceable.

Secondly, stringent credit control would be more likely to result in unemployment than would the imposition of IGT. The stop phase of stop-go operates chiefly upon the business world, in which it discourages new enterprise or makes this increasingly costly; and that kind of stagnation, if not actual contraction, inevitably spells unemployment.

But IGT has other attractions of its own. Since it would be based on the actual increase in income of every individual, it would eliminate the risk that the policy would be wrecked by the discrepancy between wage rates and earnings, which was such a stumbling block to the PIB; and, while obviating such glaring anomalies as the cases already mentioned[1] of Sir John Stratton, Mr. John Boardman and Sir John Rank, it would have the additional merit in the long term of serving as an instrument for reducing (or otherwise modifying) inequality in the distribution of incomes. Psychologically, also, restriction of incomes through statutory orders such as the Pay Code seems to evoke more bitter resentment than does loss of income through taxation. Grumbles about taxation are common enough, and workers may often be heard to complain that there is no point in working overtime if the proceeds are 'all' (which they never are) snatched away by the tax collector; yet the volume of overtime worked remains remarkably independent of variations in the levels of income tax. So, before long, deductions for income tax and for IGT might perhaps come to be lumped together in many taxpayers' minds, with the result that the one would not rouse more objections than the other.

Nevertheless the very idea of a fiscal incomes policy shocks the *Times*.[2] It would be objectionable, we are told, to 'involve our tax system, which works and is respected, in the crisis of our industrial relations'. If the miners 'can go on strike against a statutory incomes policy, they can go on strike against a statutory taxation policy for incomes, and that would be a bad lesson to teach'. Well, it has certainly not been the habit of the British to strike

1. See pp. 81-82.
2. 13 February 1974.

against taxes to which they object (the French appear
to be more so disposed) but how much weight does
this argument carry in the contemporary scene? One
may indeed hope that under a policy which restricted
all incomes alike, and not merely wages, strikes might
become less frequent; although in the last resort,
unless we are prepared to say that men and women
must never refuse to work for rates of pay which are
unacceptably low, strikes are bound to occur from
time to time. But, why should a strike against the tax
laws be more sacriligious than a strike against the
Counter-Inflation Acts? During the miners' dispute in
1973-4 we were reminded *ad nauseam* by government
spokesmen that the Pay Code had the force of law
(although actually the Secretary of State had power
to bypass it) so why is it not endowed by the *Times*
with the same sanctity as the Finance Acts? Can it be
that the top people's paper was out of date?

An IGT scheme has moreover the peculiar virtue
that it would allow scope for collective bargaining
without re-opening the door to uncontrolled smash
and grab. Collective bargaining would still be necessary because there would be no automatic right to the
maximum permitted IGT exemption. Although no
trade union leader knows exactly how much money
every one of his members takes home after all
deductions, officials engaged in wage bargaining must
have a general idea of the level of earnings of those
for whom they speak. Under IGT therefore they
would presumably aim at getting the maximum
possible increase that would be likely to leave most of
the workers concerned exempt from IGT, even though
a few might for personal reasons only be entitled to
somewhat less than this.

Even more important would be the function of the
unions in submitting to the SEB the claims of 'special
cases' for exceptional treatment by way of increases
above the normal figure for their income bracket. In

this they would still be playing a familiar role though in a novel setting and within new limitations. But with the universal enforcement of IGT restrictions alike on rich and poor, on employers and employed, the new framework of collective bargaining might not be unacceptable to them. Indeed might one not even hope that those communists (and supposedly left-wing socialists) who see no inconsistency between their insistence on freedom to grasp every penny that they can for their members on the one hand, and their uncompromising admiration of collectivised economies involving complete state control of wages and salaries on the other — might one not hope that even these absolutists might soften their attitude if IGT was so graduated as demonstrably to produce a progressively more equalitarian society?

And so to the crucial question: would IGT effectively hold back inflation? Obviously that must depend upon the graduation of the tax — that is, upon the determination with which permitted increases in income were in the aggregate kept in step with the growth of domestic production. While the unions are indisputably right in contending that wage costs are by no means the sole factor governing selling prices, no one can pretend that the vicious circle of wages-chasing-prices chasing-wages is wholly imaginary, or that in this respect there are not great differences between one industry and another. In November 1973 one of the mineworkers' leaders argued eloquently on television for an improvement in the position of pensioners, while simultaneously proposing an overtime ban in support of his members' claim for wages above the limits set by the Pay Code. Yet he gave no hint of recognising any possible conflict arising between the two halves of his theme, as a result of a rise in miners' wages being reflected in an increased price of coal which would hit pensioners hard, as had happened after the strike in 1972. Some weeks later forecasts were current that a 50% rise in the price of coal might be the eventual consequence of the dispute. At that prospect the hearts of many pensioners must have sunk, and they may even have dropped still further when the terms on which the dispute was eventually settled became known. IGT scales, however, would not neglect these contingencies.

But IGT would do much more than that. *IGT is not a wages policy: it is an* incomes *policy, the primary objective of which is to ensure that nobody, not wage-earner, not shopkeeper, not industrial tycoon, not speculator in houses or raw materials or currency or anything else should be able to enrich himself from the inflation so as to have an interest in perpetuating and accelerating it.* After all, is inflation an act of God (or of the devil) or is it the work of man? To what is to be attributed the unprecedented rise in price levels in recent years throughout virtually the whole non-communist world? These questions are surprisingly seldom asked. When they are, the stock answer is that if the blame does not lie upon rising domestic wages, then world shortages are the culprit; and these shortages in their turn are commonly traced to such factors as increasing demand for raw materials in the third world, or Japan's astonishingly rapid industrial development, or increased consumption of meat in cattle-raising countries where the inhabitants are beginning to eat the home-grown product themselves, instead of exporting it to the affluent world. Up to a point all this is true enough; yet such changes are much too gradual to explain the breakneck speed of the inflation. When wool doubles in price and meat increases by 40% in a year, and wheat by 25% in a weekend, when tin and zinc prices make new records nearly every week, when paper disappears from the shops and building plaster is unobtainable, one would suppose that half the sheep and cattle in the world

162

must have been stricken with a fatal plague, that every forest had been burned to the ground and all the tin mines flooded. But of disasters on this scale there is no evidence.

Price-rises may indeed originate in events which are not under human control, but inflation is perpetuated and aggravated by a human factor. On the recent scale it is only explicable as due to the deliberate action of people who like it because they make money out of it, and who in their turn are aided and abetted by the panic-buying of consumers emptying the supermarket shelves of toilet paper because they have heard on the radio that it is about to be in short supply. Certainly it is true that we cannot ourselves act directly on world prices, nor can we get our hands on the ill-gotten gains of persons outside this country who grow richer as these prices rise higher. Nevertheless there are still morals to be drawn from these happenings and lessons to be learned which are applicable to our own problems.

First is the lesson that we must change our habitual language, since language not only expresses, but also moulds, thought. It has already been observed that economists were once convinced that wages 'went' up or down in accordance with inexorable 'natural' laws which were beyond human intervention. Nobody believes that now, nor indeed would trade unions incur so much obloquy if it was still credible; but even to-day faith in a similar automatism is received doctrine in relation to prices. Nevertheless prices never *go* up of their own accord: they are always *put* up, and by somebody; and that is how it should be said. No price ever rises unless some human being makes a conscious decision to change the relevant ticket or quotation. Even if those who make these changes are responding to pressures which make their actions predictable, they are still not automata.

Once this is recognised, the prospects for controlling domestic inflation even in relation to rising world prices begin to brighten. A substantial proportion of the price we have to pay for our imports is inflated by the depreciation of the pound; and the value of the pound is supposed to measure what it will buy when converted into other currencies. So British holiday-makers go to Spain because pounds go further in pesetas than in the currencies of other countries in the sun. But holiday-makers are not the only, or even the most important, group of those who exchange pounds for foreign money. Every day, currencies are bought and sold in the foreign exchange markets of the world by people who live by making self-fulfilling prophecies about the prices of what they buy and sell, and it is by their actions, rather than by its actual purchasing power, that the exchange value of the pound is determined. If they expect a rise in sterling or any other currency, they stimulate this by increasing their purchases; and *vice versa.* And as with foreign exchange, so also with the domestic property market, inflation in which cannot be blamed on world commodity prices. Everyone can see for himself how the fortunes made in this and similar fields grow by what they feed on. But IGT, by preventing individuals from lining their pockets with the proceeds of speculative transactions could be a powerful weapon against this self-inflating inflation — and one much to be preferred to the practice of shooting speculators, to which some countries are addicted.

Even speculative transactions, however, are not the whole story. In the endless stream of price rises 'due to increasing costs', whether affecting domestic or imported products, it is difficult to believe that the prices are always raised exactly in proportion to genuinely additional costs. The temptation to add a little something extra must be overwhelming. Indeed the Price Commission itself is on record[1] to the effect that 'it was a recurrent theme of criticism throughout Stage 2 that the gross and net margin rules *guaranteed distributors a profit on inflation'*. These rules were therefore subsequently stiffened so as to allow, in appropriate cases, a reduction to be enforced in the permitted gross percentage margin of profit. But this problem IGT would resolve — or rather eliminate — by diverting the proceeds of such profiteering straight into the coffers of the tax collector.

There are indeed more reasons than one why control of prices through taxation should prove to be more effective than direct restriction as provided under the Price Code. Although the subject of price control in general is outside the scope of this book, I must confess to sharing the pessimism of Hugh Clegg when he wrote that: 'It is my belief that the importance of price control has been grossly exaggerated. An incomes policy needs price controls which can be used against cases of gross abuse. Otherwise they are of little value, and the promise of stable prices enforced by price controls is highly dangerous'.[2]

In support of this attitude I would quote, first, the sheer magnitude and complexity of any system of price control which would have sufficient coverage to be really effective. Admirable though the Price Commission's efforts are (and I write in the hope and expectation that they will be continued and improved), they are necessarily operative in a restricted field covering only the larger firms. But the twenty-one million individuals (or married couples) who are recorded by the Inland Revenue as in receipt of personal incomes do not spend those incomes solely on purchasing from big businesses. While it

1. Price Commission, Report for 1 September to 30 November 1973, p.13 (italics mine, BW).
2. *How to Run an Incomes Policy* (Heinemann Educational Books, 1971) p.45.

may be a formidable enough task to assess the liability of every one of this number for income tax, (with or without the addition of IGT), the mind boggles at the prospect of controlling the prices of all the goods and all the services that these twenty-one million consumers buy. Most of us purchase hundreds of different articles, and the shopping list of even the poorest must contain scores of items in the course of a year. What is more, we do not all buy the same things, as is immediately obvious if one glances at the contents of other people's trolleys at a supermarket check-out. To give but one small individual example I myself in the past week or two have purchased (in addition to foodstuffs) a typewriter ribbon, some ink cartridges for my pen, a torch battery, some furniture polish, three books, a roll of kitchen paper, a lawn mower, and two varieties of tights and a pair of shoes; I have also renewed my subscription to a specialist journal and employed the services of a plumber, a blacksmith, a hairdresser, a laundry, a garage, a window-cleaner and a television engineer. In this collection there are only 3 articles or services which did not cost more than at the time of my last previous purchase.

Second, price regulation is all too easily defeated by simple cheating. As every housewife knows, goods not only rise in price: they also have a way of shrinking in size or quality. Where articles are sold by weight, or other precise measurement, such as coal or petrol, a check can be kept on this by a requirement that the actual quantity sold should be clearly indicated, but in how many of the articles on my list was any such check available? Looking over my own sample, I ask myself how can the Price Commission keep an effective watch on what I and the rest of the 21,368,000 income-receivers have been charged for the contents of all our shopping baskets; and I sadly conclude that comprehensive control of prices is impracticable.

I would however temper this pessimism by two considerations. First, price control can be very much more easily made effective in industries that are publicly owned than in capitalist enterprises, whether corporate or privately owned. In public enterprises no one can enrich himself by putting up his prices, and therefore no one has an incentive to accelerate the inflation. In relation to public enterprise therefore there is no place for the fantastic intellectual gymnastics which the Price Code required the Price Commission to perform in order to prevent prices being raised to levels that yielded excessive profits. Though seldom recognised or quoted as such, this is one of the strongest arguments for the spread of public ownership.

Second, an Incomes Gains Tax under which pockets could not be lined by inflation would be a most powerful instrument for putting a stop to it. It seems that we have yet to learn that *inflation is caused by inflation.*

To conclude the argument, I would like again to emphasise the following points:

1. It is just not true that what people are paid concerns only those who make the payment and those who receive it. In the case of wages and salaries, rises do not necessarily come out of the pocket of the recipient's employers: collective bargains are repeatedly paid for by consumers and/or taxpayers for whom no seat is reserved at the bargaining table. What is more, the whole community has a direct concern in the overall distribution of income, inasmuch as this shapes the social, as well as the economic, pattern of the society in which we live.

2. A century of social legislation testifies to the growing rejection of the naive doctrine that if

167

everybody is free to do the best he can for himself, that will produce the best result for us all. To socialists particularly this doctrine should be wholly repugnant and acceptance of what amounts to a policy of smash and grab in so crucial a matter as the distribution of income is an illogical anachronism.

3. The alternative to an enforceable incomes policy is universal respect for the commandment: Thou shalt do what it would be a good thing for everybody else to do. But experience does not suggest that unquestioned obedience to this commandment is anywhere attainable. If it was, we could dispense with most of our legislation relating to, for example, trade descriptions, town and country planning and road safety.

4. That being so, control over the growth of incomes should be regarded as a permanent element in any social programme; and an Incomes Gains Tax on unacceptable increases in personal income, irrespective of the source from which these are derived, but adjusted to the circumstances of the individual taxpayer, might well prove to be the simplest, the most equitable as well as the most nearly painless method of operating such a policy.

# Summary of proposals

The main proposals in this book may be summarized as follows:

1. In place of the control of incomes by the imposition of a 'pay limit' as under the Price and Pay Codes and a restriction on dividends by Order under the Counter-Inflation Act 1973, an Incomes Gains Tax (IGT) should be introduced.

2. IGT would be levied on personal incomes only, at a rate of 100% on any increase above a prescribed maximum percentage in any financial year. The aggregate increase permitted in the total of *all* incomes would be calculated so as to keep this in step with the increase in output available for domestic consumption.

3. The permitted increase in an *individual* taxpayer's income free of IGT would be related to the size of his existing income after payment of income tax and other statutory contributions. A taxpayer would be limited in any year to a percentage increase in his net income, graduated ('primary grading') so as to allow larger increases on smaller incomes and smaller increases on larger incomes up to a point at which no increase at all would be free of IGT.

4. In calculating a taxpayer's liability to IGT, certain forms of additional income such as annual increments on a previously agreed scale, or higher pay due to promotion or a limited amount of earnings

169

from voluntary overtime would be disregarded, as (subject to certain differences in detail) they were under the Pay Code in relation to the pay limit.

5. Incremental scales should be more widely used than at present, particularly amongst weekly wage-earners, since they provide regular additions to pay without adding to inflation or to the total wage-bill unless there has been a significant change in the age-composition of the group of workers concerned.

6. IGT would be administered in the ordinary way by the Inland Revenue authorities and appeals against individual assessments would be dealt with in the same way as appeals against income tax assessments.

7. It would be open to organisations representing workers or employers in a particular industry or occupation (but not to individuals) to apply for more generous increases in income free of IGT (secondary grading) than the primary grading on their members' incomes would normally allow. Similar applications could be made by the Secretary of State on grounds of the national importance of a particular industry or occupation.

8. These applications would come before a Special Exemptions Board (SEB) composed, if possible, of representatives of employers, employees and the consuming public, but in any case of persons who are well known for their public service and their knowledge of industrial relations and kindred matters.

9. Applications for special exemptions from workers' or employers' organisations should be based on evidence (1) that they were paid less than others

doing genuinely similar work or (2) that their work is undervalued as measured by some agreed standard of evaluation or (3) that the earnings in their industry or occupation are insufficient to attract as large a labour force as the national interest requires. Every effort should be made to work out agreed methods of job evaluation which could be used to assist objective assessment of evidence under (2) above.

10. Evidence that a group of workers had dropped to a lower place or stood below the average in the table of earnings should not by itself be an acceptable ground for special exemption from IGT.

11. Recommendations by the SEB that applications for special exemptions should be allowed would come into effect only if approved by the Secretary of State.

12. Additions to income from inheritance, gifts and other sources which are merely transfers of purchasing power from one individual to another should be disregarded in IGT assessments as being non-inflationary. Insofar as they maintain or aggravate undesirable inequality of wealth or income, these effects would be more suitably dealt with by changes in income tax or death duties.

13. Any necessary adjustments should be made to Capital Gains Tax to prevent evasions of IGT by additional income being treated as a capital gain and subject as such to a lower rate of tax.

14. Where a taxpayer's income has been reduced below that of the previous financial year by a spell of sickness or unemployment he should be entitled to claim that his IGT assessment should be based on the income of an earlier year.

# Index

Adamson, Campbell, 92; urges
 fairer distribution of wealth
 and income, 92
Anomalies, definition of, 74
Anomalies Report, 75
Anti-growth school, 20
Arbitrator(s): influence of, 112;
 myth of impartial, 113

Balance of payments, 15;
 increase in adverse, 15
Barber, Anthony, 12, 144
Bellinger, Sir Robert, 19
Bequests, 143
Boardman, John, 82, 159;
 increase in salary, 82
Bow Group, 56-7; Memorandum,
 56-7
British Rail, 28, 119
Brown, Lord, *see* George-Brown,
 Lord
Burns, Dr. Arthur, 64
Burton, Cecil, 103
Business profits, method of
 dealing with, 49

Canterbury, Archbishop of, 102,
 106; salary, 102, 106
Capital and income, division
 between, 144
Capital Gains Tax, suggested
 method for revising, 145, 171
Catherwood, Sir Fred, 92
Civil Service Arbitration Tribunal,
 111-12
Claims to special treatment,
 121-2
Clegg, Professor Hugh, 35, 43, 50,
 52, 83, 138, 165; views on
 Prices and Incomes Board, 50;

proposes all wage increase
 claims to be reviewed by
 tripartite administration, 52;
 opines price control importance
 grossly exaggerated, 165
Coal Board, 25, 28, 72
Coal dispute, negotiations for
 settling, 11
Collective bargaining, 11, 22,
 25-6, 28-9, 53, 55, 107, 160,
 167; issue in, 23
Combination Acts, repeal of, 27
'Comparability' criterion, 43, 45,
 47; general principle of, 44-5
Comparative pay, influence of
 social conventions on, 107
Comparisons, 86-7
Confederation of British
 Industries (CBI), 58, 115-16,
 132
Conservative Government: allows
 £ to float, 22; policy with
 regard to income increases
 and profit restraint, 35-6;
 reintroduction of statutory
 controls by, 53; devotion to
 'growth', 61
Conventions, challenge to
 established, 30
Corporate enterprises: profits
 of, 141; no attempt to be
 made to impose IGT on, 141
Corporation Profits Tax, 141
Cost-of-living arguments, 77
Counter-Inflation Act, 1973, 65,
 86, 97, 160, 169; difference
 in policy under, 67
Counter-Inflation (Temporary
 Provisions) Act, 1972, 62-3,
 86, 160
Counter-Inflation Codes, 155

Counter-Inflation policy, 22

Crossman, Richard, 57; criticism of co-politicians, 57-8

*Daily Mirror,* 153

*Daily Telegraph,* 58, 153

Deflation, 16

Department of Employment's New Earnings Survey, 100-2; earnings of non-manual workers, 100-2

'Differential' system, 54

Differentials, 114, 158

Discrepancy between negotiated wage rates and actual earnings, 44

Dividends: analogy between restrictions on wages and, 48; method of dealing with joint-stock, 49; Treasury authorized to restrict, 68-9

'Early warning system', 38

Earnings: 'league table', 101, 121; disregard of status in, 126

Economic revolutions, 11

Economy, 'overheating' of, 21

Electricity Council, 119

Electricity Supply Industry, Tribunal's Report on, 24-5

Equity, 85

Ezra, Sir Derek, 103

'Failsafe mechanism', 55

Fairness, 111, definition of, 109

Feather, Victor, *later* Lord, 25; identifies unions with public, 25

*Financial Times,* 152; rise in index, 18

'Fiscal', 88

Fiscal incomes policy, 159

'Flexibility margin', 75

Freeze, unequal operation of, 63

Fringe benefits, 107

Gas Corporation, 119

George-Brown, Lord, 36

Gray, Dr., 157-158

Growth, 16, 17-21; Conservative Government policy of, 17, 61

Heath, Edward, 57, 61-2, 85, 109; outrages unions with series of budgets, 57-8; proposes incomes policy modelled on Eire system, 61-2; announces failure to reach agreement with CBI and TUC of voluntary counter-inflationary scheme, 62; states necessity to bring statutory measures, 62; proposes anti-inflation policy modelled on USA, 63-5

IGT Special Exemptions Board (SEB), 130-2, 155, 170; objects of, 130-1; membership of, 131, 170-1; possible governmental representation on, 131; task of, 132; function of, 132-3; procedure, 133; financial position of, 133

Impartial arbitration, 110-12; naive faith in, 110-11

Incomes: contractual, 34; 'other' as inflationary, 35; personal, 85-6; control of growth of, 168; additional, 171

Incomes Data Services, 70

Incomes Gains Tax (IGT), 88-9, 93-8, 135-62, 164-71; exemptions under, 89, 95-6, 122-3, 125, 130, 131, 135-7, 141, 147, 154-5, 160; three substantial advantages of, 96-8; graduation of, 99, 138, 146, 149, 161, deciding claims to special exemption under, 130; disincentive effect of, 137; alternatives to, 139; standstill imposed on substantial incomes, 140; relations with Capital Gains Tax, 143; examples of hypothetical cases, 148-51; as viable policy, 152; income controlled through Inland

Revenue, 153-4, 170;
appeals against, 153-5; counter-
inflationary effect of, 158;
other attractions of, 159;
allows scope for collective-
bargaining, 160; restrictions
of, 161; as an incomes policy,
162
Incomes policy, 34, 36; statutory,
32, 143
experiments in, 86; voluntary,
32, 37-8; public familiarized
by successive governments,
84; criterion of fairness to be
incorporated into, 109;
criticism of working through
tax system, 152; alternative to
enforceable, 168
Industrial Conciliation and
Arbitration Tribunal, 112
Industrial Relations Act, 58
Industrial Relations Bill, 57
Industries; relative position of
different, 101
Inequalities of wealth and
income, 94-6
Inflation, 22; as cure for
deflation, 16; curing i. by
inflation, 17; wages as likely
contribution to, 33; IGT as
possible brake on, 161-4;
caused by inflation, 167
Institute of Personnel Management,
128
Investment, difficulties
distinguishing between
genuine and fictitious, 142

Jackson, Tom, 29-30, 55
Job evaluation procedures, 127-9
Job transference, 135-6
Jones, Aubrey, 35, 59, 123,
125-6; recommends
re-establishment of a Prices
and Incomes Board, 59;
criticizes separation of
powers, 66; Works, *The New
Inflation*, 35q.
Jones, Jack, 30
Jellicoe, Lord, 66

Jenkins, Clive, 68, 108
Joseph, Sir Keith, 91-2
Juveniles, anomalous position
of, 146

Keynes, John Maynard, 1st
Baron, 13-14, 142; Works,
*General Theory of Employment,
Interest and Money*, 13q.

Labour Election Manifesto 1974,
55
Labour Government: 'Joint
Statement of Intent'
regarding growth in profits
and wages, 36-7; surrender to
statutory control of incomes,
37
Labour Party: leaders' distaste for
statutory controls, 52-3; 'great
compact' with TUC, 53;
advocates direct statutory
action on prices, 54; reverts
to distrust of compulsory
policy, 56; failure of statutory
policy, 61
Labour shortage, 125; used by
trade unions in pay claims, 124
Lacey, Robert, 102; investigation
into take-home pay by, 102-3
Land, cost of, 19
Language, habitual changes in,
163
'Latest increases', 70
Lawton, Lord Justice, 79;
judgement by, 79-80
'Leap-frogging', 122
Levin, Bernard, 92; advocates
equality in society, 92
Liberal Party: commitment to
statutory policy, 58; proposal
to introduce anti-inflation
tax on prices, wages or
dividends, 152-3
Low pay, definition of, 71-2

Males, weekly earnings by full-
time adult, 12
Manpower: distribution of under
Stage 2, 72; situation of in

industry, 124

Maudling, Reginald, 57; accepts need for statutory controls, 57

Mine(r)s: wages of, 24; drift of men away from, 119; nature of m. work, 119

Miners' dispute, 1973-4, 80-1

Mitchell, Joan, 45

Monopolies Commission, 32

Morris, Robert, 103

National Coal Board, 119

National Incomes Commission, 36

National Institute of Economic and Social Research, 35

National Opinion Polls Market Research Ltd., 103; survey regarding wage relativities conducted by, 104-5

National Savings, increased investment in, 19

National Union of Mineworkers, 25, 72

'Natural law', 105

Net income, distribution of after income-tax payment, 90-1

New Society, 84; survey for, 84

Nixon, Richard, 64; abolishes Pay Board and Price Commission, 64

Oil shortage, 12

Opinion Research Centre, surveys by, 84, 92-3

'Other incomes', 38; control of, 37

Output, increased rate of, 20

Overtime, 137: contractual, 137; voluntary, 137-8

Pay Board, 20, 28, 65-7, 72, 97: not authorized to recommend rates of pay, 68; requirements of, 69; unimpressive record, 69; principles under Stage 2, 69-71, 79; powers of, 79; role in miners' dispute, 81; comparison with Prices and

Incomes Board, 83; empowered to restrict any remuneration, 97; Report on Relativities, 107; Report on 'wider relativities', 113-18, 124, 133; entrusted with authority to settle relativities, 117-18; Report's analysis of miners' work, 119-20, 130; not given principles to work to, 121; adds Appendix on Job Evaluation to Relativities Report, 128

Period of Severe Restraint, White Paper on, 126

Personal income, sources for increase in, 143

'Phases', 63-5

'Plus rates', 44

Price Commission, 20, 65-6; efforts of to control prices, 165-6

Price control: preventive influence of IGT on, 142; magnitude and complexity of, 165-6; defeated by cheating, 166; more effective in publicly-owned industries, 167

Price rises: higher wages as factor for, 23; origination of, 163

Prices and incomes, standstill on, 38

Prices and Incomes Act, 1966, 38-41, 47, 48, 138; penalties for infringement of, 51

Prices and Incomes Act, 1967, 38, 41: extends deferment period on adverse Board Report, 41; penalties for infringement of, 51

Prices and Incomes Act, 1968, 38, 42, 48: deferment period extended, 42; penalties for infringement of, 51

Prices and Incomes Board, 39-40, 59, 77, 132-3: constitution and functions of, 37, 113; acquires statutory status, 39; independence of, 39; Reports, 40; Prices and Incomes Act,

1966, lays down explicit instructions as to criteria governing pay and prices decisions, 40-1; status upgraded by new legislation, 41; closure of, 42; produces Report on *The General Problems of Low Pay*, 43; produces Report on Railways Pay, 43; Report on Pay of the Industrial Civil Service, 43; General Reports of, 44-6; attitude to distribution of manpower influenced in national interest, 46; *Report on the Pay and Conditions of Busmen*, 47; chary of permitting exceptions under comparability criterion, 47; gives overwhelming predominance to control of prices and wages, 47-8; poor record of containing inflation, 49-50; decides wage claims within certain prescribed principles, 50; actual achievements, 50; miscellaneous list of Reports, 51; complex situation of effect of wage-rates on distribution of manpower, inability to handle, 73; restriction in controls and power, 78-9; comparison with Pay Board, 83; claim as independent and impartial agency, 109; categories considered as exceptional cases, 122-3; 'similar' work used as criterion in pay-identification out of line, 126; Reports examine schemes used in Europe, 128

Primary grading of IGT, 89-90 93, 109, 113, 122-3, 129, 132-3, 169

Productivity or payment by result schemes, 122, 138-40

Profiteering eliminated by IGT, 165

Profits and profit limitation, 68

Property values, enormous inflation of, 18-19

'Public interest', resistance to conception of, 24-6

Public services, low pay in, 124-5

Public's valuation of occupational pay, 104-5

Rank, Sir John, 82-3, 159; increased salary of, 83

'Reference level', 140

'Reflation', 15-16: definition of, 17; period of, 17

Relativities: definition of, 114-15; problems of, 115-19; as main standard employees judge fairness of pay, 126

Relativities Board, 72, 81, 130, 131

Retail price index, increase in, 63

Review Body, 108, 155

Ricardo, David, 105; doctrine, 105

Robens, Lord, 92

Robinson, Derek, 73; suggestion regarding manpower and wages problems, 73

Rookyard, Marilyn, 103

Saving, difficulties distinguishing genuine and fictitious, 142

Scales, incremental, 136, 170

Scanlon, Hugh, 30

Schultz, George, 64

Secondary grading of IGT, 113, 121, 170

Secretary of State, 132; function of in determining relativity problems, 115-16

Self-employed persons: incomes of, 37; assigned to Price Commission, 86; position of in relation to IGT, 140-1

Severe restraint, period of, 39

Share prices, all-time high attained, 18

Shareholders, 48

Social factors as determinant in income pattern, 108

'Social justice', 87, 90, 111

Social Science Research Council, 35

'Special cases', 122-4, 132-3, 160; person's reduced income, 145-6, 171

Speculative buying, as reason for share prices' high level, 18

Speculative gains, 144; liability for IGT, 144

'Stages', 66: Stage 1, 70, 74; Stage 2 Code, 67-8, 70-1, 74, 75, 79, 83, 86, 88, 108, 135, 137, 139, 147
imminent demise of, 73; failure of, 78
Stage 3 Code, 68, 71, 73, 79, 81, 83, 86, 88, 114, 121, 135, 137, 139-40, 147
becomes operative, 74-7
Stage 4, 113

Standards of living, no advance in, 54

Statutory taxation policy, 159

Stewart, Michael, 32; pamphlet by, 32-3; view of regarding incomes policy, 33

Stock Exchange booms, 18

'Stop-go' formula, 15-16; 'Stop' phase of, 15, 158-9

Stratton, Sir John, 81-2, 159; increase in salary, 81-2

*Sun, The,* 58; proposals by, 58

*Sunday Times,* 102-3, 106

Surtax analogy, 141


'Threshold arrangements', 76

*Times, The,* 53, 57, 92, 152, 159

'Trade cycles', 13-16; theories regarding, 13-14

Trade Union leader: role of, 27-8; salary, 28; cordial relations with employers, 28

Trade Union Movement, 27-8

Trade unionism: idealization of, 27; growing strength of, 28

Trade unions(ists), 13; changes of outlook among, 30

Trades Union Congress, 20, 25, 55, 58, 115-16, 132; 'social contract' with Labour

Government, 84

Unemployment: continued rise in, 15-16; alternative to, 20-1

Unions: contemporary, as organized representatives of sectional interests, 29; function of in submitting 'special case' claims, 160


Voluntary cooperation, 37

Voluntaryism, 58


Wage claims, 11-12; 'rounds' of, 11-12

Wage differentials, 106; between similar and dissimilar work, 126-7

Wage increase 'rounds', subject to uniform restrictions, 54

Wage reductions, 12-13

Wages: control of, 33; as likely contribution to inflation, 33; changes in level of, 33-4; 'fair' settlement of disputes, 113

Weems, William, 103

Wilberforce, Lord, 11, 24-5, 111: Inquiry, 1971, 24-5, 111; Inquiry, 1972, 119, 120

Wilson, Harold, 21-2, 53, 57: announces devaluation of £, 22; states Labour Party's rejection of statutory wage controls, 53-4

Winsbury, Rex, 32; pamphlet by, 32-3; views of regarding incomes policy, 33

Woodward, Christine, 103

Wootton of Abinger, Baroness, 34-5; proposes comprehensive Incomes Gains Tax (IGT), 88-9, 93, 94-5; Works, *The Social Foundations of Wage Policy,* 34q., 35q., 99q.

Workers: possible exploitation of, 27; claims of to special treatment, 135

Working hours, reduction in, 21

'Working Together Campaign', 103, 105

177